T0272411

Praise for *Immortal Truths* and Ravi Tewari

"A didactic collection of fables that should be read by aspiring leaders on their ascension of the corporate ladder. The lessons within will resonate with the reader for a successful life."

–Ronald Harford, former Managing Director
and Chairman, Republic Bank; author

IMMORTAL TRUTHS

RAVI TEWARI

IMMORTAL TRUTHS

TIMELESS WISDOM *FOR* CAREER SUCCESS

Forbes | Books

Published by Forbes Books, Charleston, South Carolina.
An imprint of Advantage Media Group.

Forbes Books is a registered trademark, and the Forbes Books colophon is a trademark of Forbes Media, LLC.

Printed in the United States of America.

10 9 8 7 6 5 4 3 2 1

ISBN: 979-8-88750-110-9 (Hardcover)
ISBN: 979-8-88750-111-6 (eBook)

Library of Congress Control Number: 2024900288

Cover and layout design by Lance Buckley.

This custom publication is intended to provide accurate information and the opinions of the author in regard to the subject matter covered. It is sold with the understanding that the publisher, Forbes Books, is not engaged in rendering legal, financial, or professional services of any kind. If legal advice or other expert assistance is required, the reader is advised to seek the services of a competent professional.

Since 1917, Forbes has remained steadfast in its mission to serve as the defining voice of entrepreneurial capitalism. Forbes Books, launched in 2016 through a partnership with Advantage Media, furthers that aim by helping business and thought leaders bring their stories, passion, and knowledge to the forefront in custom books. Opinions expressed by Forbes Books authors are their own. To be considered for publication, please visit **books.Forbes.com**.

To my dearest family,
my wife Lisa and my daughters Mia and Sophie.

Contents

Introduction

Almost everyone wants the best outcome for their career and their life. They study hard, work diligently, and make a lot of personal sacrifices. It is always wonderful to see such people succeed. It fulfills our sense of justice. The reality though is that much of the time these people do not succeed, at least not fully. They do not achieve the career, financial, or personal goals that they want, so they study more, work harder, and make more and more personal sacrifices. Too often this still does not lead to the desired outcome. They become frustrated and perhaps even a bit bitter. It is painful to see good, honest, hardworking people fall into this pattern. It causes suffering. Unjust suffering. Not only to them personally but also to others around them, as it can taint their management style, their inter-office relationships, and their personal relationships. The aim of this book is to show that by making slight changes to how we approach acquiring knowledge, working hard, and making personal sacrifices, we can prevent much of this suffering and be more successful.

This book is not about me but about the observations from my thirty-year career on what leads to success and what does not. To give the subject matter context, I have had a good career and life so far. God has been good to me, sometimes I think more than I deserve. My father died when I was quite young, but I was raised by a loving mother. I grew up in a middle-class neighborhood in Port of Spain, the capital of Trinidad and Tobago. Of significance is that Trinidad is one of the most cosmopolitan countries in the world. The diversity of races, ethnicities, and religions is amazing. Equally amazing is the level of cohesion. In interacting with each other, differences in race, ethnicity, and religion are treated as absolutely irrelevant. Because of this attitude, I have the benefit of seeing issues from many different perspectives.

I blossomed in high school because the atmosphere was enriching to my mind, and I was making lifelong friends. My grades were good enough for the government to pay for me to attend Bayes Business School in London, England, to study to become an actuary. I loved my time in England. The most important lesson that I learned there was that people are people! Most people, no matter who they are, have an inherent goodness and kindness within them. I graduated with a first-class degree, and I had offers to work in London, a city that I had come to love. But I chose to return to Trinidad, because I also loved Trinidad. Trinidad had made me who I was, and I felt that I wanted to contribute to making Trinidad a better place.

I spent my career in the financial services industry. At first I worked as a consultant, then as a manager, executive, and eventually as the CEO of quite a large insurance company with operations in more than twenty countries in the Caribbean and parts of Europe. My career progressed quickly. I was a manager by my mid-twenties, an executive by my early thirties, and a CEO by my mid-forties. Along the way I have been blessed with a fulfilling marriage and two wonderful daughters.

I realize that people have formed theories about why my career moved so quickly. Some believe that it was because of my ambition. That's not true, however; I am only moderately ambitious. Some believe that it was because I am hardworking. I am hardworking, but there are many people who are more hardworking than I am. A few believe that it was my intellect. This cannot be it. Many people are smart intellectually and in different ways. If I happen to be smart, I know that it is nothing very special.

I have come to realize that the reason why my career progressed quickly is because I look at things just slightly differently from others. If we are lucky, as children we are taught that to be successful, we should study, work hard, and make sacrifices. These three things are powerful virtues and are always, in some form or fashion, the bedrock of success. What we are not taught, however, is that in pursuing these virtues, we have a tendency to form certain attitudes that are counterproductive because they undermine our success. *I must be right all the time! I must be the victor in my negotiations! The more knowledge I acquire, the better I will perform!* Notions like these, which are not always true, flood our thinking.

We also tend to underestimate the value of small changes to how we approach our career and life, though they often have massive impacts on our success. Very little is written about these small changes in approach, as they do not lend themselves to academic study. And yet, they are powerful and timeless truths. Practices like making people feel safe, not falling in love with our ideas, and seeing the world as it is, not as we want it to be.

As I reflect on my career, I can recall many instances where I have seen people achieve rich and well-deserved fulfillment and act with the best of humanity. However, sadly, I have also seen too much suffering. I have seen too many good people work hard and make sacrifices yet not progress in their career. I have seen people with "holes in their heart" and toxic management styles that, apart from ruining corporate performance, more importantly have destroyed the happiness and sense of fulfillment of their employees. It is this desire to lessen suffering in the corporate world that has motivated me to write *Immortal Truths*.

I believe that life is the best university. There is so much to be learned from simply observing the world. That is why each chapter begins with a story of characters from history and mythology that should be slightly familiar. There is at least one lesson within each of these stories. The lessons have nuances and subtleties that are best understood through the vehicle of a story. The second part of each chapter is an exposition that develops the lesson conveyed in the story.

This book often speaks of how the mind works, what the definition of intelligence is, what behaviors derive the best outcomes, and what the true drivers of success are. I have the greatest of respect for academia, psychologists, behavioral scientists, and economists. This book is not meant to contradict them nor tread on their territory. It conveys observational knowledge based on thirty years of observing how people think and behave in the corporate world. Simply put, this book is derived from studying what works and what does not work.

Once again, my hope is that this book, in at least a small way, reduces the level of suffering in the corporate world. My wish for you is that it leads to better work, a happier personal life, and to a career that is more successful and more fulfilling.

Cristobal Errs to Succeed

Why Being Decisive Is Better
Than Being Perfectly Correct

Our image of historical characters tends to be frozen at a particular age.
Christopher Columbus (a.k.a. Cristobal) was once young, too. We know that
in his youth he worked as a sailor, that he would one day marry Filipa who
lived on the island of Porto Santo, and that there once existed a fantastic
spice called silphium of Cyrene. Perhaps there is an untold story about
how these elements intermingled and planted an idea in the mind of young
Christopher Columbus, an idea that would lead to great discoveries ...

I t's a warm summer morning as Cristobal and Barros walk along
the cobbled harbor of Porto Santo Island. Barros is nervous as,
encouraged by Cristobal, they have slipped away from their duties
offloading the goods from their ship that docked in the harbor that
morning. As young sailors, life and wages were not bad aboard the
Flor de la Mar. Barros did not want to upset the captain.

"Come, Barros. The shipwright at the harbor told me the way to
the Pico," says Cristobal in his charming voice as he walks quickly ahead.

"The only tree grows on Porto Santo Island at the top of a hill called
Pico do Castelo. It is ancient. The last of its kind," the old spice trader

had said to Cristobal when he was in Lisbon, Portugal, a few months before. He was referring to a tree that produces silphium of Cyrene, an ancient spice treasured by Roman gourmets as a delightful enhancer of meat dishes and as an exotic perfume. It had long been thought to be extinct, and according to legend, the last of it was consumed by Emperor Nero during one of his many bouts of madness and debauchery. The thought of finding a source of silphium tantalized young Cristobal. This rarest of spices would sell for a king's ransom to the aristocrats in Lisbon.

As they approach the top of Pico do Castelo, they discover to their consternation that the dusty road ends at an imposing iron gate set into high stone walls. On the side of the mountain, they notice a lonely shepherd tending to a small, scrawny herd of sheep. Approaching the shepherd, they make inquiries about the owner of the estate enclosed by the walls.

"Senhor, that is the estate of Don Fernando Perestrelo. He owns all of the land as far as you can see."

"I must see him," says Cristobal firmly.

"I do not know how, senhor. He is not a nice man. Cruel. We hardly see him except when he summons us if we are unable to pay him his rent. Or when he rides on horseback to the port to board a ship to travel to one of his other estates."

Leaving the shepherd, they walk slowly back toward the road. Cristobal, lost in thought, gently kicks pebbles as he moves down the path. Suddenly Cristobal starts to walk briskly toward the wall.

"Cristobal, we cannot go in there!"

"There is a tree here. We can use it to climb over the wall!" shouts Cristobal as he shimmies up the tree. Barros pauses, thinks twice, and decides that he will follow his friend.

They create a small cloud of dust as they jump to the ground on the other side of the wall and quickly look around cautiously to see whether they are alone. No one is in sight. In the distance at the very top of the hill, they see a large baroque villa surrounded by a well-kept garden. The landscape is arid with dusty soil interspersed sporadically with thorny shrubs. There is little natural cover, but as they move toward the villa, they do their best to stay concealed by staying off the footpaths and behind the low shrubs.

"Where is everyone?" whispers Barros.

"Luck favors us, my friend. I do not think that Don Perestrelo and his men are here. They must be off collecting rent. But we must be quick. The tree is at the top of the hill, so it must be around the villa."

As they approach the villa, they realize that there is life within. Some of the windows are open. Through one of them, they can see what looks like a kitchen and the glimpse of a kitchen maid. The aroma of a stew permeates the warm air. They hurry through the garden to the wooded area to look for the silphium tree.

As they search the entire area, their hearts become heavy. All the trees are young and of familiar types. Prosaic fruit and ornamental trees.

"Cristobal, we have to leave before we get caught. The tree is not here!"

"It must be," says Cristobal, his voice lacking its usual confidence.

"What must be?" says a female voice.

Startled, they turn around. Before them is a beautiful young girl, her green eyes in delicate balance against her olive skin and radiant brown hair.

"What are you thieves doing here? This is my father's land. He will kill you for trespassing."

As she ends her threat, the sound of hooves echoes in the distance. They all realize that Don Perestrelo and his men are returning.

"No, menina, wait. Please! We are not thieves. We are just looking for a tree."

Her eyes soften slightly as she looks at Cristobal.

"You fool. You risk your life for a tree."

"Please, there must be an ancient tree near to the villa."

"Fool, my father cut away the old forest to create this garden. I remember it from when I was a young child."

Cristobal's heart would have sunk, but in her glow it instead sang.

"I can see you are not thieves, just fools," she says. "Leave before my father punishes you. There is a small gate on the other side of the hill."

"Menina, before I go, what is your name?" Cristobal asks.

After a slight pause, she says, "Filipa," then as she turns away, "now go quickly."

Following Filipa's advice they scurry to the other side of the hill where they discover the small gate. It is unlocked. As they briskly walk back down the main road, Barros grumbles. "That was a total waste. The captain will be upset, I am sure."

Cristobal does not respond. He is lost in thought.

As they pass the shepherd, he calls out, "Did you find what you were looking for, senhor?"

"Not quite," responds Cristobal. Barros casts him a confused look.

"You are lucky to be sailors. I wish I could sail around the world like my grandfather did. We used to be great sailors once. Now we are just poor shepherds."

"I have been called a fool three times today, but I can see that you are the fool, shepherd. How can you sail around the world? If you sail too far west, you will fall off the great ocean."

"That is not true, senhor. If you sail to the edge of the world, there is another edge. And if you sail to that edge, there is yet another one. My grandfather sailed until he found new land. He said you could keep sailing forever."

Barros laughs. Cristobal contemplates. They leave the shepherd and hurry back to their ship. In his head, Cristobal is oddly excited, but he does not know why.

Did something deep inside Cristobal know that this was not the last time he would see Filipa, that she would be his future wife? Did it know that in being wrong about the spice on the hill, he received the seed of an incredible idea that the world was, in fact, round? Perhaps it even knew that this was not the last time his mistake would lead to wonderful discoveries.

 People say that I have had a successful career. I could have been more successful, but there is objective truth to this. I became an executive very young. I went up the corporate ladder to senior positions relatively quickly. I retired young. I changed every company I ran, for the better I hope, and I have never run a company where I did not at least triple profits well within ten years. But I will tell you a deep, dark secret. I cannot recall ever being right, not even once!

That is not to say that I was never right. I assume that I was right some of the time, maybe even most of the time. But I am also equally convinced that I was wrong a lot of the time. To me, what is important is not about whether you are right or wrong; it is about moving on and getting things done. Just as Christopher Columbus moved on when he was completely wrong about the existence of the spice tree on the hill. He gained something from his misadventure, the idea that the world was round. He did not focus on being wrong. He discarded his mistake but retained the knowledge that it created.

What does "right" mean anyway? Too many people suffer from the "polar fallacy"—they believe that every issue, every situation, and every interaction can be broken down into polar opposites, two incompatible extremes like the two poles of a magnet. They believe that something is either good or bad, or hot or cold, or right or wrong. Under this fallacy, nothing can exist in between these polar opposites. Social media reinforces this, although in a neurotic fashion. Sometimes it tolerates large ambiguity between right and wrong, but at other times it severely punishes someone for a single mistake. One mistake can cast a lifelong shadow. So, we are conditioned that it is always better to be safe—to be right—than to make a mistake.

Of course, good and evil and right and wrong exist, and of course in many moral and ethical circumstances nothing can be tolerated in between those polar opposites. However, most of the time in real-world decision-making, that is not how life works.

What is "right" depends on context. Is it right to go for a walk carrying an umbrella? Maybe it is if there are clouds in the sky. But maybe it is not if you like to sing and dance in the rain. Maybe it is if you are ill, but maybe it is not if you are healthy. The point is that most of the time there is no absolute "right" or "wrong." You need to develop the conviction to do what you believe is right given the circumstances. Many people shy away from this simply because they overestimate the adverse consequences of making a wrong decision. This leads them to be very slow in making decisions to the detriment of their life and their career.

I challenge you to do an exercise. Look back at your life over the past year, which should be relatively fresh in your memory. Now pick out some decisions that you would say were right decisions and pick out some decisions that you would say were wrong decisions. When I ask people to do this exercise, in general they find it much more challenging than it seems. And in trying to do so, they tend to fall within two different groups.

The first is those who find it difficult to recall individual decisions, and even when they do so, they feel ambiguous about categorizing the decision as either right or wrong. In doing the exercise, they realize that over the infinite span of time, the validity of individual decisions pales into insignificance. When they consider decisions that might be construed as "right," they can see that while they were right, they were not perfect. They also realize, however, that while not perfect, the decisions they made were functional and took them forward and created progress. When they consider decisions that might be construed as "wrong," they realize that, in the vast majority of instances, things worked out in the end because they corrected course, or that things can still work out, because it is not too late to correct course.

The other group will much more readily identify decisions that they see as right and decisions that they see as wrong. However, they too realize that in the infinite atmosphere of time, in most cases, each individual decision is nothing but a mote of dust. They realize that, in hindsight, the decisions they viewed as "right" were usually not perfect and that "wrong" decisions were usually inconsequential or have already been corrected.

The point of the exercise is to reveal that if we study the consequences of making decisions it reveals that the vast majority of the time making a perfect decision is unnecessary and making a wrong decision is inconsequential.

Being right all the time comes with a heavy price—the price of speed. Most things in the universe, including when it comes to certainty in a decision, obey the Pareto principle, or the 80:20 rule. You can get to 80 percent certainty relatively quickly. But to be right all the time you need to be 100 percent certain, and getting from 80 percent certain to 100 percent certain takes a long time. It is a slow meandering process. Like most things, certainty jumps from zero to eighty but crawls from eighty to one hundred. Effective people simply cannot function this way. Success and slowness are mostly incompatible. Exact precision is not always necessary. The context of the task in question, however, should be carefully considered if at all possible. Knowing the circumstances of the situation gives you more room to intuit the question of choosing precision or usefulness: "Do I need to complete a task perfectly, or do I simply need to be useful right now?" Performing a brain surgery, for example, requires precision, while composing a first draft for a presentation only requires one to be useful and efficient with their time and anyone else's who may be involved.

There is, of course, a more subtle, more insidious price to being right all of the time—the destruction of some human relationships. Pathologically needing to be right prevents us from seeing the other side. We hold on to half-truths. We become defensive and strike out to protect our position.

The question is then, how can one be effective and make quick decisions in a universe that is naturally uncertain? The solution comes from the realization that to be effective is not about how often you are right, but rather how quickly you recognize that you are on the wrong path—and how efficiently you pivot to get back on the right one. In the story, Christopher Columbus was wrong to believe what the old spice trader told him about the existence of the spice, but he realized that he was on the wrong path when he met Filipa and stopped trying to find the long extinct spice. Along the way he gained knowledge that the world was round and that became his new path.

In the world of rock climbing, there is an expression known as the three-foot rule. In essence, the adage reminds climbers not to approach a climb with the full rock wall in mind, but rather to focus on it in three-foot sections. By focusing only on what you can reach with your hands and feet, you force yourself to solve smaller, immediate problems. To make quicker, smaller decisions and to learn and correct quickly. As a result, you can reduce the chances of becoming overwhelmed by the enormity of the problem in its entirety. I'm not a rock climber personally, but that philosophy can be extrapolated to just about anything outside of climbing a giant rock.

We live in the fast-paced world that rewards speed. We are faced each day with a myriad of decisions to make, and we often must make them quickly. It is easy to experience what's known as decision fatigue, which I'll discuss in greater detail in a later chapter. Don't be afraid of making the wrong decision. It is inevitable, given the sheer number of choices we must make every day. Just focus on the range of options directly before you and choose one. You can correct your direction later if needed. It is much more productive to walk in a path that might be slightly wavy than it is to have a lengthy debate before taking every single step.

It is important for everyone to learn the skill that every good sailor knows—to keep moving while gently correcting course. To not be afraid of wavy lines, as often they are more productive than dead-straight ones. The universe is not cruel. The vast majority of the time the decisions you're faced with are not existential ones. When they are, you are aware well in advance. We are all hardwired to know when our existence is under threat. Many times a slight detour, as Cristobal's futile search for an extinct tree, leads to a wonderful, life-enriching discovery. Welcome the adventure.

The path to success is to constantly be in motion. It means embracing the fact that every step may not be perfect, but that in every step we get closer to our destination. It is to quickly correct our course, and to have a sense of appreciation for mistakes, because within every mistake, there is a lesson that creates an opportunity to learn and become better.

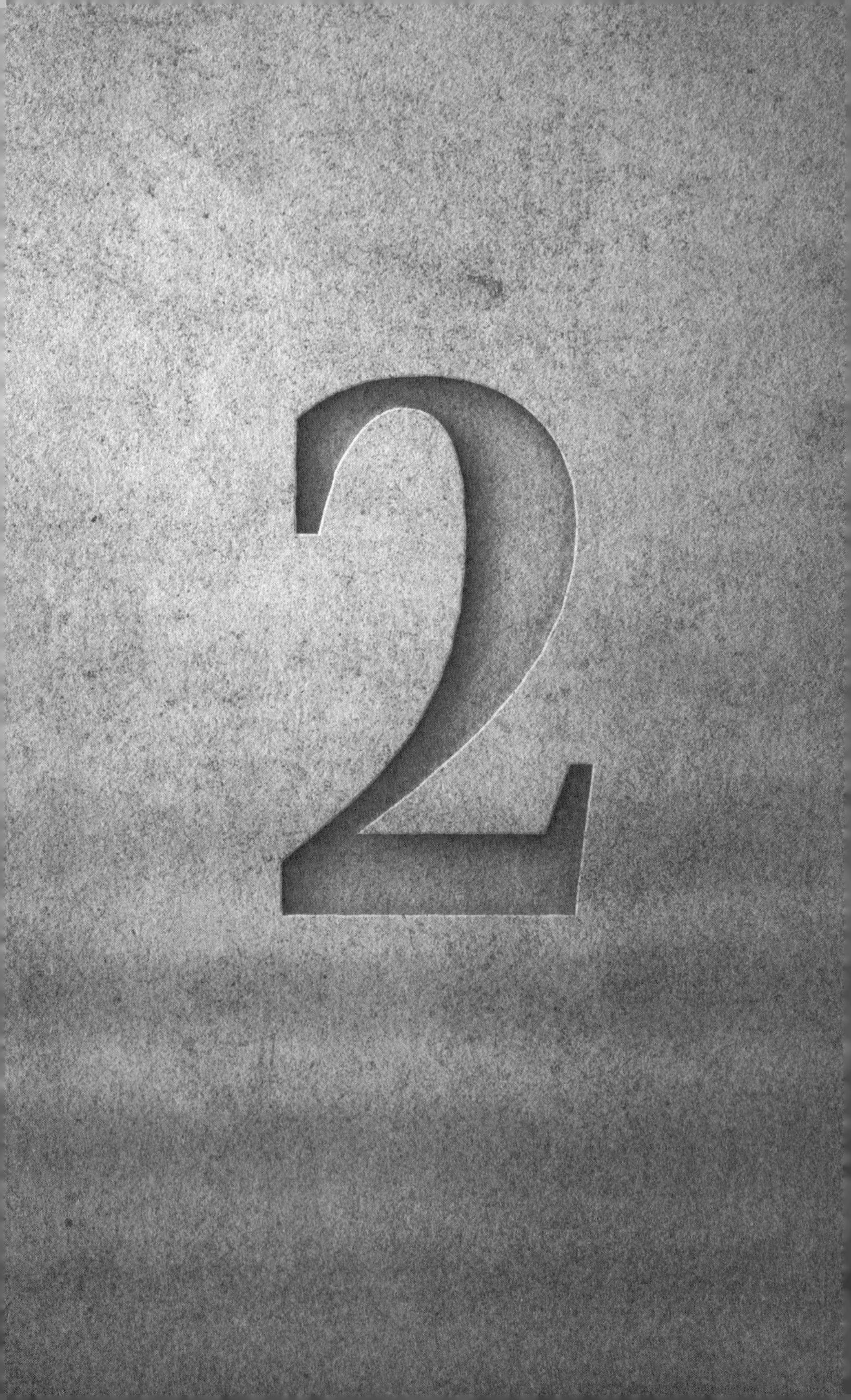
2

Sir Walter Knows

The Power of Knowing That You Don't Know Everything

Sir Walter Raleigh, born in 1552, was an English aristocrat and adventurer who contributed to Britain's rise as a world power. He was a favorite of Queen Elizabeth I, though he fell out of favor and was beheaded by her successor James I. He was obsessed with finding El Dorado—the lost city of gold. On his expedition to search for El Dorado in 1595, he visited the island of Trinidad to use the pitch from its Pitch Lake (a lake not of water but of pitch) to mend the hulls of his ships. El Dorado has never been found. What if he missed a vital clue from a humble boy during that visit ...

Jibacoa walked along the muddy path toward the sea. He could see the fleet of caravels anchored in the distance. The midday rains having recently stopped, he could feel the heat of the tropical sun beating down on his bare back. His shoulder ached from the weight of the basket that he was carrying. Sticky black pitch oozed through the weaving of the basket and burned his shoulders.

He lost count of how many times he had made the journey between the caravels and Pitch Lake over the past few days. He enjoyed both ends of the journey. At one end, the sight of the English caravels with their lowered sails limply fluttering in the wind was magnificent. At the other end, Pitch Lake was a magical place to him with islands of flowering trees floating on an expanse of black pitch that, though technically liquid, was so thick that someone could walk on it. Thousands of hummingbirds hovered over the lake, creating a cloud of iridescent greens and blues. The English used the pitch to mend holes in the hull of their ships. In Jibacoa's mind, this act was the sailors feeding medicine to ships wounded from the long journey across the ocean.

As he approached the caravels, he heard an authoritative voice behind him.

"Boy, come here!"

Putting his basket down by the shoreline, he turned to see a tall Englishman, surrounded by lightly armed men. The Englishman appeared to be their leader; although his shirt was smeared with dirt, it was of better quality than that of the other men. His dusty face had a softness to it.

"Come quickly!" shouted one of the men. "Sir Walter Raleigh wants to speak to you," gesturing toward the Englishman.

Jibacoa cautiously approached Sir Walter.

"My men tell me you speak our language. How is this so?" questioned Sir Walter.

"A priest lived here once, sir. He taught me, but he is dead. Fever killed him in the wet season."

"Thank you for bringing the snake-stone yesterday. It saved my sailor's life. It stuck to the wound and sucked the venom out of him."

"There are many snakes here."

"There are many snakes where I am also going. I must have more snake-stones. Bring more to me, and I will give your people more cloth and knives."

Jibacoa quickly agreed. Cloth and knives were precious to his people. His tribe had been working for weeks to supply provisions to the caravels in exchange for what was precious to them. The opportunity to earn more in exchange for a few snake-stones made Jibacoa happy.

When Jibacoa returned to deliver the snake-stones that night, he was led to a makeshift tent. Sir Walter Raleigh sat at a desk studying a map under the light of a lamp. Jibacoa offered him the snake-stones.

"Only five?"

"That is all we have, sir. We trade for it with a tribe from over the sea, but they have not come for a long time."

"Very well," muttered Sir Walter. He realized that the tribe must have reserved some for their own use, but that matter was not worth provoking a fight.

Sir Walter gave Jibacoa a bundle with cloth and knives. As Jibacoa turned to leave, he glanced at the map. Noticing this, Sir Walter said, "That, boy, is the way to El Dorado."

"I do not know of this place, sir."

"I know everything about it. I have been studying it for most of my life."

Sir Walter explained that he had first heard about El Dorado in his youth from a Jesuit priest, who had attended a banquet at his father's estate. Noticing the keen interest shown by Jibacoa, Sir Walter told him the details of how he gained his complete knowledge of El Dorado through extensive research at all the major libraries of Europe over many years. He told about his trips to the National Archives of Spain in Madrid, as well as his adventures in remote Templar castles in the Highlands of Scotland that concealed secrets about El Dorado.

After listening to everything that Sir Walter had to say, Jibacoa suggested, "If it is a secret place, then it must be hidden in the mountains in the center of this island."

Sir Walter laughed. "My boy, the world is so much bigger than your little island. It is not on this island. It is over the sea on the mainland."

"But why do you seek this place, sir?"

"It is full of wealth, covered with everything precious."

Picturing a treasure of cloth and knives, Jibacoa said, "I have never seen such a place; it must be ruled by a very powerful queen."

"Queen!" said Sir Walter, irritated. "No, it is the capital of a civilization. Its ruler is a mighty king."

Sir Walter decided that there was no point in continuing to discuss El Dorado with Jibacoa. Although he had taken a liking to the boy and was sympathetic to him, Sir Walter rued that though Jibacoa was clearly intelligent his perspective was limited as he lived all of his life on a small island.

The next day Sir Walter and his fleet sailed off to South America. They would face many challenges and lose many men as they searched for El Dorado—a search that would prove futile. The discovery of El Dorado eluded Sir Walter his entire life. It is even said that he was muttering about El Dorado just before he was beheaded years later at the Tower of London.

The day after Sir Walter sailed away, Jibacoa and his tribe journeyed into the mountains of his island to visit their capital city and pay tribute to their queen with the precious cargo of cloth and knives for which they had worked so hard. Walking up the ancient stairs to the city, Jibacoa kicked away emerald pebbles.

As Jibacoa labored to carry his treasure of cloth and knives, he thought, "I hate these green stones; they look pretty but they are sharp and hard to walk on. And in this part of the island, they are in the soil everywhere."

Looking ahead at the gilded hall where the queen held court on a throne made of yellow metal, he wished that one day he could visit the city covered with everything precious that Sir Walter Raleigh had described.

There is a vast difference between hearing and listening. Sir Walter heard the words that Jibacoa said but he did not listen to their meaning, which was right beneath the surface. He did not listen because he thought he already knew everything about El Dorado, so he certainly could not learn anything from a native boy from a little island. The story may be fiction, but the reality is that too many people fall into a similar trap to the detriment of their lives and their careers.

Sometimes a scene from a TV show or a movie can be a very powerful metaphor of the real world. One such example is the opening sequence of *Mr. Bean*, a British sitcom from the early 1990s. A one-word description of Mr. Bean would be "clueless." In the opening sequence, on a dark street in Britain, a beam of light suddenly streams from the heavens. Instantly, Mr. Bean appears as if cast down on Earth, lying flat on his stomach in the circle of light where the beam hit the street. He then stands up, confused, and starts to run around randomly and completely bewildered.

The metaphor is the innocence of birth, whether this is the birth of a person or the birth of humanity itself. Any entity that appears anywhere for the absolute first time must be confused, and is completely ignorant of its environment. Then the magic of learning begins. The physics of the environment are explored. The traits and behavior of other living entities are examined and learned. Theories about how everything interrelates are formed and either confirmed or discarded. The process of learning is exponential. Discoveries build upon discoveries, and knowledge builds upon knowledge. The ability of the entity to master its environment increases steeply.

One beautiful aspect of this process is that knowledge is always useful, even when it is imperfect and incomplete. We look back at history with the perspective that knowledge has increased tremendously over time. Surely a car is more useful than a horse-drawn carriage. However, that is not to say that a horse-drawn carriage was not extremely useful to people at the time. Similarly, in the future, cars will have evolved tremendously. But that is not to say that cars are not useful today.

This is a wonderful, organic process. However, it often goes horribly wrong. It does so in two ways. One tends to affect people at the early stages of their careers, and the other tends to affect people who have risen to more senior positions within an organization.

In the real world, we do not enter any situation completely innocent and bereft of past experiences and knowledge. On the contrary, at the early stages of someone's career they enter organizations glowing with the product of years of academic study and with many past experiences. This should be very advantageous, as it allows people to get a head start in entering a new environment. However, education, whether it is academic or experiential, is a double-edged sword. For the people who realize that there is so much that they do not know, it is a catalyst for success. For those who believe that in their education they have received almost everything they need to know, it is a hindrance to development.

When Steve Jobs delivered the commencement speech before Stanford University's 2005 graduating class, he said, "Stay hungry. Stay foolish." Jobs was a college dropout, but he never stopped educating himself and learning from his experiences. Jobs knew that feedback from others is key to one's self-awareness, as well as their personal and professional progress.

It is often productive to see the merits of an approach by considering how someone would behave in an existential situation. How would the most experienced and trained soldier behave if he were parachuted behind enemy lines? Would he assume that his experience and training are all that he needs to know? Or would he first take stock of his landscape and situation and then apply his experience and training to prevail?

People work very hard for their education, and they should be very proud of it. However, as easily as an education can make someone seem like a genius, so can it make a fool of someone. The world has too many educated fools. An education in itself is not the finished product. It is a collection of tools to be applied to create finished products. Like all tools, these are not always most productively used by any standard method. The user needs to figure out the tricks and the hacks and to have the confidence to throw away the manual.

Many simple yet critical and practical things in the real world cannot be taught through a list of instructions from a textbook. Anyone who is learning to drive knows that it would be pure folly to be given a textbook on how to use a steering wheel. The concept may be explained, but some things are only learned by the application of that knowledge.

The other way in which the learning process goes horribly wrong, as tends to happen later in someone's career, is by assuming that the upper bound of knowledge is finite and that conveniently, perhaps to satisfy our vanities, we are already at this upper bound. This mode of thought is encouraged by academia.

For all the wonderful achievements and gifts that science has given to us, it suffers from the weakness of hubris. There has never been a point in time in the past where science has not assumed that it has understood almost everything about the physical world, and that this knowledge will be complete only within a few years. However, there has also never been a point in time where this assumption has been correct. Today, we laugh at some of the scientific beliefs from two hundred years ago, the same way that two hundred years ago, they laughed at the scientific beliefs of people two hundred years before their own present day. The same way, I dare say, that in two hundred years' time, our great-great-grandchildren will laugh at our current scientific beliefs.

We have always presumed that, for the first time in history, we are on the verge of mastering the physical world, but we have never been correct. Why should we happen to be right now? This is not a critique of science, nor is it arguing that science is not tremendously useful and beneficial. As I have pointed out earlier, knowledge does not need to be complete nor perfect to be useful.

Even if we can understand everything about the physical world, we cannot understand everything about an organization with people possessing an infinite mix of personalities operating in an infinite possibility of scenarios. Success within any organization is based upon mastering situations and human interactions and learning from them.

Assuming that "I already know" is often a trait of people who raise up an organization and then stagnate and never live up to their full potential. They cannot move to a higher level because they already believe that they know everything. So like Sir Walter in the story, they close their minds, do not read the signs, and never find their "El Dorado." It is a fact that in the real world the people who have the most practical insights about something are the people who practice it. Their level in an organization or their academic background is irrelevant. The people who do, know. Senior people in an organization who believe that they know best lose access to this tremendous font of knowledge. They also lose the command and respect of many within the organization, especially at junior levels. Not only do these senior people fail to live up to their potential, but so does the organization.

Let's revisit the life of Sir Walter Raleigh for a moment, who was a real English statesman, solider, and explorer of the sixteenth century. He possessed a natural curiosity and an unquenchable thirst for adventure, traits that were both great strengths in his life, but which were ultimately the impetuses of his demise.

As a young man, Sir Walter Raleigh demonstrated remarkable intellect and an insatiable appetite for knowledge. He excelled in his studies, absorbing every ounce of knowledge and wisdom he could find. His ambition and drive propelled him to the forefront of society, catching the attention of Queen Elizabeth I herself. Gifted with wit and charm as well, he soon found himself in the prestigious position of one of the queen's trusted advisors. As his influence grew, so did his aspirations, and his stomach for risk-taking. He embarked on daring expeditions to the New World, thus planting the seeds of English colonization.

With each successful voyage, his ego swelled, fueled by the admiration of his peers and the queen's favor. It was that hubris and record of achievement that led him to believe he was untouchable, even to the queen. Doubtless this belief proved fatal, as he was seen at different times by both Queen Elizabeth I and her successor, James I, as too powerful and untrustworthy, ultimately leading James I to accuse him of treason and sentence him to his death. In short, his downfall arose because he stopped learning from the social signals that his relationship with his monarch was faltering.

In life we can believe that "we know" or that "we know a bit, but there is always more to know." Having the latter attitude involves humility, which in itself is a powerful virtue. Having the latter attitude is the key that unlocks the door to a treasure of knowledge and success, the door to someone's personal El Dorado.

The Immortal
Count Will Decide

How to Go Beyond the
"Mind" to Be Decisive

*In medieval Europe, there was widespread belief in the existence
of Count St. Germain, a gentleman, scholar, and alchemist. He
was reportedly spotted by many people over a period of centuries,
and they all observed that he did not seem to age. Rumors
spread that he was immortal. If he really existed, he would have
possessed almost limitless time. We can speculate about how
having so much time affected his ability to be decisive ...*

The silver fork clattered as it dropped onto the fine china plate. Once the guests at the royal dinner realized that the source of the noise was Countess von Gregory's apparent clumsiness, they politely resumed their conversation and their meal. Many thought to themselves that the old lady must have weak hands. As she picked up her fork, Countess Helene von Gregory stared at the young man who had just sat down at the dinner table opposite to her. He awkwardly avoided making eye contact.

"Emile," the countess said to him, "how can this be?"

"Madame, sorry … my name is Eugene," he replied. "Eugene St. Germain."

"St. Germain? Emile …"

Count St. Germain stood up and hastily left the room. He needed to think, as he was in danger of being exposed. It had been almost sixty years since he last saw Helene. A pang of guilt came over him as he realized that he had not thought of her for many years. If he had, he would have presumed that she was dead. Memories of her youthful face and her lovely girlish laughter as they danced together drifted through his mind. This was one of many painful memories that he carried with him. Memories of people that he loved a long time ago. Often more than a lifetime ago.

He realized that he made an error by once again starting to call himself Count St. Germain. It had been so long since he used that name that he thought it was safe.

I must get very far away from here, he decided. If the matter of his history were pursued, there would be too many questions that he would have to answer. Too many questions, for which the explanations were unbelievable.

He had invested most of the last two years gaining the confidence of the king so that he could get access to the royal library. The king's library was legendary, containing rare, ancient manuscripts from all over the world. But the count was only interested in one book: the Taurian Codex, and he was very close to finally gaining access to it by earning the trust of the king. He thought how unfair it would be if this opportunity slipped from his hands at the very last moment. As he thought this, the count resolved that he would steal the book and take it away with him. He justified his actions by the fact that he was probably the only person in the world who understood the codex's contents.

There are occasions that called for stealth, but this, the count decided, was not one of them. This was an occasion that called for boldness. He marched up to one of the two guards at the entrance of the royal library.

"Sir, His Majesty has asked me to fetch a book for the entertainment of his guests."

"Monsieur, I only take instructions from His Majesty. My marshal will go and confirm this with the king's valet."

In the danger of his situation, the count decided to respond with bravado. "Sir, do you question me?"

A voice from behind him confidently said, "My Count, His Majesty has moved on to other vices. Come walk with me. We can return for the book at another time if need be."

He turned around to see Helene. Her body had withered, but her eyes still held the same twinkle from her youth. She held out her wrinkled hand, and he slowly took it as they walked away.

"Emile, do not lie to me. I know it is you. We were close once, although that was so long ago. I just know."

The count could not think of what to say.

"I have heard rumors over the years, you know. My aunt said she saw you once in Vienna. And my friend saw you in London. They both said you looked the same way after many years, that you had not aged. But I did not believe them. I thought they mistook someone else for you."

He remained silent.

"What are you, Emile? You have not aged. Please tell me. You owe it to me."

"I do not know what I am," said Emile. "Just a man, I think. I don't know why, but I stopped aging when I was about twenty-five. I watched my family, my brother, my sisters, and my parents grow old and die. That was more than five hundred years ago."

"I can see with my own eyes that you have not aged, Emile. You are the same young man and I have grown old," she said, turning to smile at him. "What you say has to be true. What else can it be?" On seeing her smiling face, Emile once again remembered her girlish laugh.

"When we were both young," she said, "you used to read everything about alchemy. You were planning to become the supreme alchemist. Is that why you want this book?"

"Yes, my dear Helene … yes," the count replied. "And you used to practice on your violin all day. You wanted to be the world's greatest violinist."

"One day I stopped practicing and started to play. I never became the world's greatest violinist," she shrugged, "but for years I performed in Vienna and Amsterdam. I stopped after I got married and had my children. Did you ever get married, Emile?"

"No, Helene. I never married. I think I would like to one day, once I perfect my alchemy."

Helene reflected on her own life, her days with Emile, her enjoyment of her time as a violinist, and her happy marriage. She hoped that one day soon her dear friend of old would decide that he was perfect enough as an alchemist and would finally experience the joy of a marriage and a family. She resolved to help him.

"It's not safe for you here, Emile. People may have noticed my reaction. They prosecute many for witchcraft these days. Go quickly, my dear old friend. I want you to keep safe. I am glad to have seen you one final time. Do not worry. Write to me when you find someplace safe, and I promise I will get the book and send it to you."

Emile took Helene's advice. The Count St. Germain escaped and once again established a new life. One day he received the Taurian Codex from Helene. With affection he reflected that she was always true to her word. She was so until the day she died, having done a lot of things in her long, rich life. The count is perhaps still alive with his abundance of time giving him no impetus to make decisions. In all likelihood he has not moved on with his life and is still planning to one day become the supreme alchemist.

 I am sure that most of us have heard the Cherokee story about a grandfather telling his grandson about the two wolves fighting inside everyone's head. One wolf is full of anger and hate, while the other is full of kindness and compassion. The grandson asks his grandfather, "Which wolf will win?" The grandfather replies, "The one that you feed."

I have never met anyone who did not instantly agree with the moral of this story. Some truths are self-evident, neither research nor higher authority is necessary for our belief. We just know. We instantly agree with its moral conclusion.

However, I ask you to consider a point raised by this story other than its moral conclusion. That point being that two entities can exist within our brain at the same time. In other words, the story illustrates that our brain contains many components such as our mind, our intellect, and our intuition. It also illustrates that our mind can hold conflicting attitudes and points of view.

There are many components of our brain, and to be effective at decision-making we need to use other parts of our brain apart from our mind, in particular our intuition. We also need to use the pressure of "time" to force us to make decisions and resolve conflicting attitudes within our mind. Helene, like all of us, understood that she had limited time in her life, so she decided when she had practiced enough to make a career of playing the violin and when it was time to get married. Count St. Germain had endless time so he could afford to keep practicing to become the supreme alchemist and could put off a decision to get married.

Most of us tend to place greater value on our mind than on our intuition and the other more subtle elements within our head. In current times, we are conditioned to worship the mind. We are led to believe that our mind and the mind of experts are all-powerful, and perhaps infallible. We need to be wary about this and ensure that we understand the limitations of our mind. To do so we must consider what is our "mind." The most obvious answer is "that which we use to think." However, we need to be careful about this perspective, as while it is true, it is incomplete. When we say that we use our mind to think, we really mean that we use it to do three things. The first of these is that we use our mind to examine the past. Thinking in this context is then reflecting on the past and drawing conclusions from it. The next thing that our mind does is examine our environment through our senses. It has the ability to piece together the visual, auditory, olfactory, and tactile landscape in which we exist. And finally, the mind tries to project the future, hopefully based on the past and present, but often based on fear and imagination.

A fun fact about the mind is that it is a one-trick pony. It cannot process the past and the future at the same time. Try it! Try to think about the past and the future at the same time. You simply cannot. Also, if it tries to process either the past or the future with the present, its focus on the present is extremely poor. The image of the distracted professor lost in thought comes to mind. The mind simply is not very good at processing either the past or the future. Its recollection of the past is incomplete, often inaccurate, and usually biased. Its ability to project the future falls off exponentially as we move further and further into the future. In other words, it projects imaginary futures. It does, however, have a tremendous ability to perceive the present, though this too is being eroded as concentration spans have fallen over the past few decades. Living in a world full of constant distractions while developing concentration and perception is an art that is very difficult to master.

It is clear that we have a problem here. The part of our brain that we value most for thinking is bad at two of the three things that it does: processing the past and the future. While it is good at sensory perception, this ability too is increasingly diminishing.

So how do we resolve this problem? As mentioned, the answer lies in the story of the two wolves—not so much in the direct moral, but in the revelation that there is more than our mind within our head. We must realize that our capacity to make decisions is much more expansive than just using our minds. There are so many more wonderful and magical things within our heads. Every day we tell our mind to think about different things from our past. Every day we direct our attention left, right, up, or down, not out of reaction, but out of will. Every day we imagine and we fantasize about future scenarios, though perhaps less than we used to do when we were children. Our intellect comprises more components than just our mind. And while our mind alone may be imperfect (perhaps heavily so), in totality, with everything that exists within our heads, we are as perfect as human beings can be.

The point of the above discussion is that you cannot make a decision with your mind alone. Left to itself, the mind will wallow in its incomplete recollection of past events, and it will create imaginary futures. Sometimes, in between, it will pay some attention to the present, but usually only if you force it to do so. The mind is simply not a decision-making organ. The good news is that other parts of your intellect are, whether it is your will or your intuition or your subconscious or your soul.

It is a fact that those who succeed in the business world are those who are decisive. Take as an example when someone is having difficulty with the service in a store and asks to speak to the manager. They do so because they presume that people higher up in an organization have the ability to make decisions or are able to make better decisions than more junior people. This should be an obvious clue that anyone who aspires to rise through the ranks of an organization needs to be viewed as someone capable of making good decisions. In any office, people know which colleagues to avoid because any task given to that colleague will drown in a lake of indecision.

It is sad to see so many bright, sincere, and hardworking people fail to progress in their careers simply because they use the wrong approach to decision-making. They focus way too much on what their minds like to do in collecting information and making plans. In doing so, they are not conscious enough in the present moment to seize opportunities, and neither do they have the understanding that they must use parts of the intellect other than their mind to break the inertia of indecision. This understanding needs to be combined with the message from the first chapter that being decisive is better than being correct. In other words, use all of your facilities to make decisions having considered the context to confirm that correct but imperfect decisions as well as wrong decisions (that can be rectified) are usually inconsequential in the long term.

A mind thinks that it is perfect, but it is not. It cannot gather complete information on which to make a perfect decision, nor can it perfectly anticipate every future scenario. Like Helene, becoming more advanced and successful in any field involves acquiring the judgment to know when it is time to act in the face of limited information that cannot attain perfection. It also requires the confidence to know that although every possible scenario cannot be predicted, every possible scenario can be overcome. One of the key underpinnings of success is understanding that, most of the time, any decision is better than no decision.

Hernando versus Tuskaloosa in a Battle of Hubris

| Why Humility Creates Success |

Hernando de Soto (1500–1542) was a very successful Spanish conquistador. His conquests were so successful that there was never a shortage of volunteers when he set out on a new expedition. He sought to crown his illustrious career by discovering gold in North America to rival that of the Aztecs and Incas. Tuskaloosa (died 1540) was a giant of a man by stature and respect. He was tall, muscular, and lean, the leader of many tribes and territories and feared by nations that he did not control. We wonder how the interaction went between two such proud men ...

By the time his scout breathlessly told him of a possible trap awaiting them in Tuskaloosa's prized city of Mabila, Hernando de Soto had already decided that his men's suspicions would be ignored. De Soto was certain that a mysterious city of gold like those previously discovered in the lands of the Incas and the Aztecs was just out of his reach. This had eluded him for years, thus denying de Soto the national glory that he had longed for since boyhood.

At age thirty-eight and having already spent a quarter of a century exploring, pillaging, and conquering the Americas in service of the

Spanish crown, de Soto could have returned to Spain with his wife and lived out the rest of his days as one of the wealthiest men in the wealthiest empire on Earth. But the insatiable draw to see, defeat, and accomplish something greater was too strong for de Soto.

Both the fates of de Soto and those in his path would align when captured natives reported that there were immense gold and riches lying on the lands across the waters from La Habana, Cuba, effectively turning de Soto's sights north to a vast and little-known New World.

As de Soto's expedition penetrated deeper into the territories of a network of Mississippian tribes, tensions grew. The conquistadors sought to establish dominance and gather resources, while the native peoples were wary of these newcomers who threatened their way of life.

The towering Tuskaloosa was a wealthy and powerful supreme Apalachee chief known for his intimidating size and the austere nature with which he ruled his tribe and vassals. Tuskaloosa had initially wanted good relations with the conquistadors. He sent his son as an ambassador to de Soto and invited him to his town, where he welcomed de Soto and his men with fermented brew, women, and a feast.

As the evening of uneasy festivities waned, de Soto cut to the point. In a commanding voice he stated, "I will need porters to carry supplies and enough food for my men, as well as women."

Tuskaloosa was not used to receiving commands. He recipro-cated, "I am not accustomed to serving anyone. In turn, all serve me."

That night de Soto outnumbered Tuskaloosa both in men and in guns. He ordered that the chief be detained and kept under guard in the palace the Apalachee had provided the visiting governor. Rather than immediately engaging in conflict, Tuskaloosa decided to go through with his previously planned strategic game. With his majestic fortress-city of Mabila as the center of his influence, Tuskaloosa planned to lure de Soto into the city. Tuskaloosa knew that a direct confrontation with the well-armed and mounted Spanish cavalry was a daunting prospect, so he devised a plan to exploit the city's labyrinthine layout to his advantage. He ordered four hundred men to serve as porters for de Soto's expedition and promised de Soto that he would have one hundred "most desirable" women and food for him at Mabila.

This all seemed too convenient to many of de Soto's men, including his top advisors. They advised that the better course of action would be to negotiate with Tuskaloosa. "Tuskaloosa would bend to my will!" was de Soto's reply.

The pivotal moment arrived on a fateful day in October 1540, when the Battle of Mabila erupted. As de Soto and his guards entered the city, they were greeted with music and singing alongside gifts of blankets and furs. Tuskaloosa and a local chief then led them to the city's center where three to four hundred Apalachee gathered with fermented beverages, music, and "marvelously beautiful women" whose exotic dancing diverted the attention of the visiting Spaniards.

Meanwhile, Tuskaloosa slipped away to a hut where his military leaders were holding a council of war. A large number of warriors allied to Tuskaloosa were delayed in arriving to Mabila. The question before the council was whether to wait for the warriors or to spring the trap shorthanded. Tuskaloosa, his patience fraying and ego swelling under the indignity of having to submit to de Soto any longer, ordered his men to attack immediately.

De Soto had already noticed Tuskaloosa's absence and signaled to his guards to rush the hut and extract Tuskaloosa with force. Before they could enter, de Soto and his vanguard realized they were already victims of a carefully orchestrated trap. They looked around and saw that the houses were not empty as assumed but in fact each one was filled with dozens of Apalachee warriors, now emptying out around them. De Soto grabbed his helmet and sword and drew first blood by hacking off the arm of a nearby Apalachee warrior.

Suddenly the narrow streets and hidden passageways of Mabila became a battleground, as Tuskaloosa's warriors launched a surprise attack from all sides. The small group of Spanish soldiers were cut off from the rest of their forces that lay sprawled along the Alabama River. Chaos ensued as the two forces clashed in the streets, with de Soto trying desperately to keep his men together. There was a nearby gate through which he could have escaped, but this was not de Soto's way. Instead, he mounted a horse and abruptly led a charge directly into the midst of the unarmored attacking force, thereby creating a path for his remaining guards to follow. The men battled their way through the fray and out of the city's main gate to a surrounding field where they raised the alarm among the other soldiers.

The fighting was fierce but in the end, the Spanish emerged victorious at a great cost of lives. The city lay in ruins, and Tuskaloosa's power and his people were shattered. Estimates of Apalachee deaths range in number from the hundreds to the thousands, making it the bloodiest European-Amerindian battle in North America up to that point. Tuskaloosa himself disappeared but was believed to have been burned beyond recognition during the battle.

With its leadership wiped out in a single night, Apalachee society fell into decline. Two decades after the Battle of Mabila, another Spanish expedition encountered a small group of Apalachee among the ruins of a once-great civilization. They eked out an existence as hunter-gatherers as opposed to their sophisticated ancestors.

As for de Soto and his surviving men, they would winter near modern-day Tupelo, Mississippi, to lick their wounds before continuing their search for gold. Though de Soto's forces were significantly battered and weakened his arrogance was intact. He again demanded some two hundred porters from the local Chickasaw, who in turn also attacked the expedition causing de Soto and his men to flee the area to the Mississippi River. Shortly after crossing the mighty river, a battered de Soto died on its western bank of a fever.

The relationship between de Soto and Tuskaloosa showcased the collision of two strong-willed, arrogant leaders from two vastly different worlds. The Battle of Mabila left a lasting impact on both the Spanish and Indigenous peoples, serving as a reminder of the hubris that shaped the early interactions between the Old World and the New.

 In a world often dominated by ego and the pursuit of conquest, it is easy to overlook the influence that humility provides: from good and effective leadership to just being a happier, more contented person overall. To cultivate humility someone must be on guard against its diametric opposite, hubris or vain overconfidence and arrogance. This is often the nemesis that may be silent to you but glaring to others. It's the deciding factor that can swiftly erode the authenticity that you may represent to others.

Humility is a concept that seems to have eluded leaders like Tuskaloosa and de Soto. It is not about self-deprecation or lack of confidence but rather about being in touch with the reality that so many people in myriad of small and often invisible ways play a part in each of our successes. Humility involves understanding that success is subjective, it is personal, and no matter how successful we are, it does not diminish whatever has been achieved by others. That we are mortal and that in the vastness of time we and our achievements become the dust of ages. Humility is a genuine recognition of our limitations and an openness to learning and growth.

A humble leader is approachable, relatable, and adaptable. When you're humble, you become more approachable to your team. Your humility signals that you're not above others and that you value their input and perspectives. Team members feel comfortable sharing their ideas, concerns, and even mistakes. This open dialogue fosters creativity and innovation.

Humble leaders are relatable leaders. They connect with their team on a personal level because they're not afraid to show vulnerability. Soto and Tuskaloosa feared any chance of looking weak or incompetent in front of those under their command, so much so that they could not admit to nor correct their errors even if it meant stubbornly marching on into fatally wrong decisions. But sharing one's own challenges and setbacks can humanize you in the eyes of others, which can actually build deeper trust and respect among those under your leadership. If you share your own growth journey, including times when you've learned from your mistakes, it will inspire your team to embrace their own learning experiences.

Everyone appreciates feedback and acknowledgment when they do something right or well. A leader who expresses such gratitude not only fosters a positive work environment but also motivates their team to excel. Recognizing and appreciating your team's efforts is a cornerstone of leadership. It's a simple yet effective way to boost morale and productivity. When team members feel valued, they are more likely to go the extra mile.

Any person who shows gratitude builds strong trust and loyalty among those around them. An effective leader understands the strength that a culture of gratitude can bring to their team, and they often build this culture by setting examples of gratitude themselves and encouraging others to express their thanks as well.

Usually leaders who lack humility miss the opportunities to acknowledge others, as they focus on boasting about their own achievements and on promoting themselves rather than paying attention to the contributions from their teams. Team members resent leaders who constantly take credit for successes and deflect blame for failures. This lack of accountability damages relationships and team morale. You cannot build trust with others unless you take responsibility for your mistakes and share credit generously with your team when it is due.

Leaders who possess humility are also more adaptable because they change course when warranted as they do not let their ego cloud their judgment. Unlike de Soto and Tuskaloosa they consider each piece of advice on its own merit and do not have a bias to acts that will enhance their own image. They listen to feedback, even if it challenges their initial plans.

While humility and gratitude are powerful leadership attributes, hubris is their archnemesis. Just as we saw from the story of Tuskaloosa and de Soto, arrogance and an inflated ego can be a leader's downfall.

Hubris blinds leaders to their own flaws and limits their ability to learn and grow. They become closed-minded, believing they already have all the answers. Leaders consumed by hubris often resist change, as they believe that their way is the only way. This can lead to a stagnant organization that fails to adapt to evolving market conditions. This stagnation almost always leads to poor decision-making and missed opportunities.

A subtle feature about hubris is that it can be contagious, especially at the senior management level. This manifests in the attitude of "everything that we touch must become gold," even though there has never been nor will there ever be anyone akin to King Midas. I have personally seen hubris poison C-suite executives and boards causing the loss of hundreds of millions of dollars.

As a leader, humility and gratitude are your secret weapons. They empower you to connect with your team on a deeper level, motivate them to excel, and build unwavering loyalty. However, beware of the hubristic trap, for it can undo all your good work. Strive to be the humble and grateful leader your team deserves, and you'll find your path to success is paved with the trust and admiration of those you lead.

The Gorgon, the Goddess, and the Girl

| How Not to Become a Monster |

In Greek mythology, Medusa was a dreaded Gorgon with hair of serpents and eyes that would turn anyone who looked into them forever into stone. Andromeda, the beautiful fiancée of Perseus, was being held captive and the goddess Athena advised Perseus that he should use Medusa's head to turn Andromeda's guards into stone. It is said that when Perseus was able to behead Medusa in battle, he never looked into her eyes directly. Instead he looked at her image reflected off the inside of his shield. Perhaps there is more to the story ...

Medusa could hear the whisper of his light footsteps. She could feel his movements and smell his fear. She knew who he was: Perseus, son of Zeus. She had watched him from the slits in the walls of her dismal lair as he approached. As a Gorgon and the daughter of a sea god, her senses were well beyond that of a human. She heard him speak to his crew as they sailed toward her island. She heard him say that he must go alone to behead her on the advice of his patron, Athena. A Gorgon's head, he told them, would turn his enemies to stone and allow him to rescue Andromeda.

She heard the fear in the voices of his crew. "She will fix you in her stare and turn you to stone too, my captain!" one of them said. "She has done this to many others."

"Do not worry," said Perseus. The subtle weakness of his voice betrayed his inner thoughts, though he tried to appear fearless to his crew. "I will look at her face only through its reflection on my shield. Look how I have polished the inside for the task."

Medusa did not often smile. It felt unnatural to the ancient Gorgon, but she did so when she heard these words.

All humans are greedy, arrogant, and foolish, she thought. *Humans have attacked me for thousands of years, and he thinks no one before has tried to see me only through my reflection.* She laughed menacingly. *My stare is my stare, directly or reflected. This fool too shall perish.*

As she slithered through musty, dark passages toward the scent of Perseus, her thoughts fell onto her childhood. They often did. She had existed for so long that thoughts of the past filled her head, leaving little room for thinking of the future. Her childhood was so long ago, when the world was still young.

She knew what the storytellers said about her past, and she hated humans even more for this. *Lies. All lies. The humans are so arrogant that they want to claim who I am. They like to say that I was born a human.*

The storytellers said that she was a beautiful priestess of Athena once, who out of Athena's jealousy was turned into a Gorgon. Medusa knew that this was not true.

The thought of Athena brought some warmth to her icy heart. She remembered vividly her distant childhood when Athena, her aunt, goddess of war, craft, and wisdom, would play with her. She remembered the smile of her mother and the games she played with her two sisters on their isolated island. They were cautioned by Athena that their destiny was to remain on the island separate from humans. They were entirely different from humans, Athena had told them, as even their very gaze would turn humans to stone. They accepted this destiny. All she felt now was loneliness, but back then on that isolated island, she never felt alone. Gorgons were naturally solitary creatures, so her mother and sisters were enough company. Their days passed in laughter and peace punctuated by visits from Athena. Then the world encroached.

She remembered the first time her powerful ears heard mortal voices miles away. She did not understand their language then, but she could hear the anger and hate in their voices. They came to her home with spears and swords and fire. She could not understand why her mother and sisters turned their backs to the army of humans. She watched as they were mercilessly slaughtered. But Medusa was always a fighter. A born warrior. The blood of her aunt, Athena, goddess of war, coursed through her veins and she was determined to fight. She crushed a group of soldiers with her serpentine tail and grabbed a fallen sword in each of her powerful Gorgon hands. With those swords and her petrifying gaze, she slaughtered the entire army.

Laughter and light left the Gorgon's heart. After the slaughter, Athena came to console Medusa, to grieve with her. She pleaded with Medusa that war should not be her destiny, that a Gorgon's heart needs to be filled with love not hate. This made Medusa furious. She shouted, full of venom and terror, that Athena was wrong. That she was given a gift by the gods not to spare humans from her stare, but to use it to rid the world of them. She decided that she was born with nothing in common with humans for a reason. With an icy stare, she told Athena that she would never understand why the goddess of war would not avenge the death of her mother and sisters. She turned her back on Athena and walked away.

Leaving the island, the mighty Gorgon unleashed her vengeance and fury on the world. Villages, towns, entire armies, and even nations perished under the intensity of her wrath. Mankind itself was decimated, until suddenly and to everyone's surprise she would only attack when provoked. Sages wondered if perhaps she too was mortal, and over time, she had grown old and tired. They did not know that Medusa stopped her attacks neither out of age nor exhaustion, but out of her love for a child.

I have killed tens of thousands of men mightier than he and yet he thinks he can slay me! thought Medusa as she moved toward the entrance to her castle. *Why does Athena favor him as she once favored me?* Medusa asked herself. She felt uncomfortable that she and this mortal shared Athena.

She listened to his very last words to his comrades as he entered her castle. "I must face Medusa and win. I cannot bear to see Andromeda suffer. To save her I must get the Gorgon's head."

He loves an Andromeda, too? pondered Medusa.

"Andromeda!" Medusa remembered the words fading from her victim's mouth, the last words of a mother as she was turned into stone. Everyone else in the village was already dead except an infant girl hugging the leg of the pristine stone statue. The little girl, Andromeda, turned and stared at Medusa with tearful eyes, yet she did not turn to stone. For the first time, Medusa was forced to look into eyes made not of stone but of flesh—living human eyes. Medusa was overwhelmed with the emotions flooding into her mind. As her confusion faded, she realized that the child's eyes did not possess the gift of sight, yet within them the Gorgon saw fear and bottomless grief. Medusa saw humanity in the child and, though a Gorgon, she found humanity in herself. She gently picked up her Andromeda with powerful arms that had spent eons doing savage deeds. She took the blind child back to the island where she spent her own childhood and raised and loved that Andromeda as her own daughter. That was a very long time ago.

Medusa replaced the love of Andromeda's lost mother with that of her own. She watched over her Andromeda as she grew up and lived a full, happy life. The life of a human is short compared to that of a Gorgon. One day after death claimed her precious Andromeda, Medusa retreated to a long-abandoned castle to live out her life in solitude.

For centuries, Medusa lived in the castle hiding from the world. When Perseus spoke about Andromeda and Athena, it made memories of her own Andromeda and the very same Athena flood into Medusa's mind. She laughed within her mind that she had these things in common with this human. *Maybe we are not so different after all. If he is doing the will of Athena, it must be for a pure cause,* thought Medusa.

Medusa could hear and smell Perseus. He was unaware that she was just around the corner from where he was stealthily advancing. She looked at the ancient swords that she held in each hand. They were her trophies from countless battles that she had won. Energy animated the locks of her hair and they writhed like serpents. Medusa sprang forward. As she rounded the corner, she thought of Athena, her beloved Andromeda, and the happy emotions of her distant childhood. Her last thoughts were of serving Athena, of helping someone else's Andromeda, and of realizing that she did indeed have something in common with humans. She dropped the swords and closed her eyes.

Every business enterprise is conscious of having to satisfy three very different groups of people. These are the providers of capital, the providers of labor, and the providers of demand for the products of the business. In other words, shareholders, employees, and customers. It is often overlooked that there is a fourth group of people, the society within which the business exists. At the very least the impact of the business should be neutral to its society, but ideally it should enrich it. This may be viewed as altruism, or it may be viewed as enriching the market in which the business operates for calculated gains. It does not really matter how you view it, as the impact is the same. If a business damages society, however, it is a parasite in the worst sense of the word.

Actions speak louder than words. Although the public statements of most companies will suggest otherwise, their actions, especially those of larger companies, would reveal that generally the bias is toward satisfying providers of capital ahead of employees and customers. I stress on the word bias, as I am not suggesting that most companies ruthlessly ignore their employees and customers for the benefit of their shareholders. Nor am I suggesting that this bias is necessarily a bad thing, as long as the bias is slight. The reality is that, if at all times a company endeavors to simultaneously satisfy shareholders, employees, and customers, then at no time would it totally satisfy any of these groups. The company would descend into mediocrity, neither good nor bad with no wow factor.

One of the arts of leadership is to, at any instant, give particular and intense focus to one of the groups, while ensuring that on average over a period of time, all groups are roughly equally serviced. This is not an easy task as it involves having to make very difficult decisions and compromises. It is often a matter of judgment.

In the story, for long periods of time Medusa had no moral challenge with doing horrible things to humans because she forgot she had anything in common with them. She wielded power mercilessly. Like Medusa, a leader disconnected from those they are charged with leading can grow callous and reckless, figuratively turning everyone around them into stone due to their lack of empathy.

I recall a time in my own career as CEO when I noticed myself thinking with "Medusa's head." It was a few weeks before Christmas, and I went to a toy store to purchase some gifts. I noticed someone who worked in my organization purchasing presents for his children. Unknown to him, I had been told that after New Year's he was due to be terminated. That moment made him real to me. He was no longer a name on a sheet of paper. He was a father who, like me, was working hard to provide a good life for his family. That realization triggered my creativity as a manager, and I found a way to save him from termination while still achieving the company's targets. He is still working for the company today and has grown from strength to strength.

We have all collectively created a world that is constantly changing in pursuit of progress. A cynic once told me that this implies that the world is unhappy with itself as no rational entity will want to consciously leave a state in which it is happy. Of course, this philosophical debate is outside of the scope of this book. The point is that as the world changes, things can rapidly become irrelevant and obsolete, especially businesses. Very often, this involves making changes to a company that results in the termination of employment of some people. Sometimes there is an element of self-infliction due to the poor performance of the person involved. However, at other times, this condition does not exist. Every day across the world good, productive people lose their jobs. Life is certainly not always fair.

We tend to glorify a leader as a creator, but this is only one side of the coin. Abetted by most leaders themselves, we tend to gloss over the other side of this coin. Leadership is a responsibility, a duty, and sometimes a burden. A leader is responsible to various degrees for the well-being of many people. To truly discharge this responsibility, there are times when a leader must find the strength to be a destroyer as opposed to a creator. Sometimes a wonderful new creation can only arise out of the ashes of destruction. This is ancient wisdom, replete in the myths and religious scriptures from every part of the world. The issue for a leader is how to be a destroyer without becoming a monster. The world does not need any more monsters.

The talisman to protect a leader from becoming a monster is to care. You simply cannot be a good leader unless you care deeply about the people that you lead. Everyone loves their families equally. The rich do not love their children more than the poor. Over my career I have had the privilege to do some projects with the police. From this I realized the fact that even hardened criminals love their children immensely. They do not want their children to lead the dangerous criminal lives that they do. When as a leader you fire people, you cannot dismiss the possibility that you may create hardship for them and their families. You cannot dismiss that you can create a lot of hurt. This is meant to bother you. This is meant to burn a piece of your soul every time you do it. You are meant to worry for the people whose lives your decisions will affect. This is what being a human is all about.

It does not mean that you abdicate your duty as a leader to balance all interests and act fairly in the greatest good to the best of your ability. Sometimes good, decent people need to be terminated in the interest of the business including that of the remaining staff. However, when you make such difficult human decisions, you must do so with a sense of responsibility, consequence, and care. This attitude will shape how you operate and often lead to better decisions. Behaving in this manner is not just for the sake of others. It is for your own sake, too. Your humanity is priceless.

There is an invaluable side benefit of fostering empathy. It has to do with the art of negotiation. Any effective leader needs to be able to negotiate with anyone whether that person is an ally, an adversary, or even an enemy. An inferior leader often claims that they cannot achieve a goal because of the lack of support from someone else who holds the key to unlocking their goal. This can happen some of the time, but it rarely happens to a competent leader. They understand that when you look at history, you see that people have struck deals with adversaries and enemies on innumerable occasions. If you look at current affairs, you see that opponents are striking agreements all of the time. Achieving compromise and support to move forward is one of the core duties of a leader. If a leader cannot do this, they are a poor leader to the detriment of their organization.

The magic of negotiating agreements is not to look for differences but rather to search for commonalities. What does your side have in common with the other side? If the other side is an enemy, then perhaps it is not much. But if you peel back the layers, you will come to a very deep layer that you share. Once you understand that everyone loves something, you will instinctively start to look for the highest thing that you both love. This always exists. Like Perseus the human, Medusa the Gorgon loved the goddess and they each loved a girl called Andromeda.

We were all born with a sense of caring and, for our own sake and that of others, we have a responsibility to make sure that it does not grow dormant.

6

The Bread Seller
of Old Cairo

The Amazing ROI from Giving
More Than for What You Are Paid

During my career, I have had the opportunity to travel a fair bit, and I have noticed that most people from every country are genuinely kind, willing to be helpful, and give out of pure goodwill. This includes people from countries considered "poor." People with little to give still try their best to be kind and giving! This universal, inherent goodness within the human spirit has always touched me deeply. I have realized that very often people from "poor" countries have a wealth of happiness because they have such a positive attitude. This is the only story in the book that is not based on history or myth. It is inspired by my visit to Cairo and brings out the power of kindness ...

I shan looked at the river with annoyance. A riverboat full of tourists was powering upstream, the drone of its engines dissolving any hint of tranquility. For Ishan, the Nile had changed too much over the years. It was barely recognizable as the same river of his youth. Though his body was wrinkled and worn, the old man still had keen eyesight. A subtle movement caught his attention, and he looked downriver to see two feluccas—small, single-mast sailboats—slowly sailing in the wind. The grace of these traditional vessels always hypnotized him with their triangular, white sails and brightly colored masts. Ishan was hungry, as he often was, and this made him sleepy. As a cool, morning breeze gently brushed his face, he drifted into a memory about when he was a teenager more than seventy years ago …

The souks, or markets, were the hubs of old Cairo. They were full of life. They were cauldrons that brewed experiences, both good and bad. They were alive with the din of shoppers haggling with merchants who sold an amazing assortment of objects, some of necessity and others of desire. The alleys were filled with the bright colors of carpets and cloth and the scents of spices and perfumes. Above all the sounds and sights, it was the scent of freshly baked bread that captured Ishan's senses. The scent brought mixed emotions. It held the promise of nourishment but also a sharp reminder of how hungry he was. If Ishan had time to spare it a thought, he would realize that he could scarcely think of a time when he was not hungry. The money that he earned at the souk was barely enough to keep him fed.

At his back, he could feel the heat of the dirt oven and hear Farid, the stall's owner, tossing the flat, circular rolled dough into the oven to bake them into aish.

"I warned you already, boy!" shouted Farid fiercely. "You are rolling the dough too big. You are giving away my money.

"You are a stupid boy. You do not understand business. That is why you will always be poor," he continued.

Ishan apologized as he always did. He felt that he was very different from Farid, and thought that it must be because he was just a poor, stupid boy. He was afraid to upset Farid, as he needed the pay and selling bread was the only thing in his life that made him happy. He would mostly see the same people every day or every few days as they came to buy fresh aish.

Farid did not permit him to say more than a few words to the customers. That was not his place. His place was to work. But what Ishan was not allowed to say with words he said with a smile, with a nod of his head, and with how he gently handed the customers their aish.

Later that day a little girl with bare feet visited the stall. A ragged, coarse shawl framed her dirty face. Her long shift-dress was frayed and smeared with dust. Ishan had never noticed her before. She handed him just enough coins for one aish. He could see hunger in her face. She looked at him only briefly as he gave her her purchase. As she turned to walk away, the aish slipped out of her small hand and fell onto the filthy ground. She quickly bent over to pick it up.

"No! That's OK. Leave it for the dogs," Ishan said, as he held out another aish to her. She looked into his eyes, surprised. They grew slightly wet. Ishan realized that she did not expect this, that she did not expect kindness. He wondered how often, if ever, she had come across kindness in her short life. She smiled with her lips and with her eyes, thanked him, and quickly walked away.

As he watched her walk away, a strong arm grabbed Ishan by his shoulder and dragged him out of the stall.

"You thief! That was not yours to give. She is used to eating off the floor. She is a dog!" Ishan saw fury in Farid's face. "Go away. I will not tolerate you anymore!"

As Ishan walked away despondently, he passed by an antiques stall, or more accurately, a stall that specialized in goods looted from ancient tombs. The owner had seen what had happened. He muttered, "You are a stupid boy. Farid gave you a job and you lost it for a beggar."

"Do you need someone to help you in this stall?"

The merchant laughed.

In the afternoon heat, Ishan, hungry and with no money, made the long walk home toward the outskirts of the city. As he walked farther and farther from the souk, the neighborhoods went from comfortable to destitute. At the edge of the city, he came to al-Qarafa, the City of the Dead, a series of massive cemeteries that was home to the living as well as the dead. Here the extreme poor with nowhere else to go made makeshift dwellings among the graves. Long ago, the residents would look forward to occasionally discovering artifacts among the older graves. These would be sold to tourists through the antiques stalls where they were often passed off as being far older than they really were. Those days were long gone, as all the graves were already looted.

His home and only possession was a blanket that he left and collected each day from one of the residents who was too old to leave al-Qarafa. He thought that he was blessed to own it, as it kept him warm at night. He also thought that he was blessed to live in Cairo as it seldom rained, so he did not have to worry about staying dry.

Ishan walked past the edge of al-Qarafa, much farther than he usually went. He wanted to be alone. He sat on a ledge of rocks and reflected on the beggar girl and how she did not expect to receive kindness. As his foot pressed against some rocks, they gave way and Ishan noticed that they covered a tomb. He realized with excitement that this tomb was almost completely covered, so it must be unopened. He wondered if it contained artifacts of value, perhaps great value.

Ishan paused as he decided what to do next, then performed his second unexpected act of that day. He gathered stones and used them to completely cover the tomb. As he did so, he thought of his parents lying in peace somewhere in a paupers' grave. He thought that everyone deserved to rest in peace ...

"Grandfather!" the little girl shouted with a giggle. Her voice shocked Ishan out of his slumber. As he looked toward her across his patio, he could see the feluccas in the distance behind her. In the few moments that he was lost in thought, half asleep, they had made good progress upriver.

"Breakfast is ready, Grandfather."

Ishan held her little hand and walked toward the back door of one of the finest homes on the banks of the Nile. Just before entering the house, he looked up at the sky. As he often did, he thanked God that life had been kind to him, that he had managed to save enough to open his own bread stall at the souk. He was grateful that his customers from when we worked for Farid remembered him and came in droves to his stall, helping to grow his business from that tiny stall to the largest bakery in Cairo.

He sat at the table for breakfast and thought of the little beggar girl who taught him so long ago that he was indeed very different from Farid.

 I grew up at a time and in an environment where I had nothing but the deepest of respect for my teachers. It was not a matter of liking my teachers, although I liked the vast majority of them. It was a matter of gratitude. I felt that anyone with something to teach me was in a very real sense my superior, and I was grateful that I had the opportunity for them to pass on their knowledge and experience to me.

I attended a high school with a lot of history. I saw it and still see it as more of an institution than a school. That is why I would never forget what I saw when I walked through its gates for the very first time. I was very surprised when I saw a smartly dressed teacher diligently sweeping the corridor. He saw confusion in my eyes and said politely, "Well someone had to do it; it's dusty and all the new kids are coming in today."

At that moment, I learned a few life lessons that have served me well and ones that I will never forget. I learned about humility and about getting the job done. However, there was an even deeper and more powerful lesson. I knew that this teacher was not there to sweep the corridor. Like most people would, he could have chosen to complain about the dusty corridor, but instead he chose to sweep it himself. He was paid to teach not sweep corridors; yet, like Ishan the bread seller, he did more than he was paid to do out of pure goodwill.

Over the years, thinking about that incident, I realized that by his selfless act, the teacher gained something that money could not buy. He gained my deepest respect and because of this, for my entire life, I knew that I would be inclined to be supportive of him and favor him. What an incredible return on investment a few seconds of selflessness can have! This is so even though the outcome itself was totally unintentional at the time. He was just being a decent human being, doing the right thing. The universe is indeed bountiful; it is a fact that doing the right thing pays handsome rewards.

I am sure that almost everyone would have heard the story of the airline that saved millions of dollars by removing one olive from each of the salads served to its passengers. This was universally praised by the media as an example of how good management can quickly reduce costs. However, the issue is not so straightforward. While in this context it was probably good management it would not be so in every context. At its core, this action was the transfer of wealth (the olives) from the passengers to the airline. Nothing was created; something was just taken away from the customers. Believe me, people are not foolish. They know when something is being taken away from them. So there was the potential for the creation of significant ill will, as this action was exactly the opposite of the teacher giving more than he was paid to do.

There are different classes of assets. Some assets directly impact the quality of your life—your home and your car, for example. Some assets help you to generate more wealth, such as shares in companies, investment properties, and mutual funds. Other assets give you peace of mind like money in the bank, retirement savings, and life insurance. However, do not underestimate the power of intangible assets like goodwill and respect. Whether it is at a corporate level or an individual level, these are the assets that keep on giving. The story illustrates the impact that this had on the success of Ishan's bread business. They influence how favorably you are treated, how easily opportunities open up to you, and how easily you are forgiven if you make a mistake. For an employee, these things directly impact the rate at which you rise up the ranks of an organization. They are the differentiators that shape a career.

We tend to call this intangible asset "brand." I do not like that term as it is too often misused. It has become associated with cheesy advertising and making false promises. It tends to give the impression that to gain the assets of goodwill and respect, one needs to invest heavily to promote oneself and to promise more than can be delivered. Nothing can be further from the truth. Goodwill is not earned by self-promotion. It is earned by selfless acts.

Gaining goodwill does not cost much. In fact, it does not have to cost anything at all. What is required is that in everything you do, do just a little bit more than is expected. It costs nothing or very little to give a customer a smile, to spend an extra few minutes to make sure your report looks beautiful, or to draw a smiley face on a package that you deliver. I cannot begin to tell you all of the ways that you can practice this, because it is specific to what you do. You do not even need to do it all the time, just a lot of the time. You do not have to worry if you are noticed because over time you will be.

You do not have to worry if people are ungrateful because enough people will be grateful.

I generally believe that it can be a very dangerous thing to do something that affects other people just to make yourself feel good, as well intentioned as you may be. However, this is not the case here, so long as what you do is not imposed on other people but instead treated as a gift.

I suppose that you would expect me to now say that in whatever job you are doing, you should practice what I have said so far in this chapter. I would like to stress: No, no, no!

You need to understand that some parts of many organizations are broken because someone there has risen to a position of authority who does not have any inclination to do more than for which they are paid. If you report to such a person, your actions will only be seen as a threat. Your quality of service will make your supervisor insecure. If you are in such a position you have two choices: you can either wait and hope that the organization will fix itself, or you can move on to a different position or organization. The latter is usually better in the long term. You should not suppress the valuable person that you are. A functional organization will value your attitude, and you will be tremendously rewarded for it, not necessarily immediately but in the long term. Giving more than that for which you are paid is one of the key ingredients of success, in terms of career and in human relationships.

7

Leonardo's Compromise

The Art of Knowing When to Use Different Forms of Intelligence

Leonardo da Vinci will always be remembered as one of history's greatest geniuses. He was not just an academic genius but so too was he a creative and artistic genius. He was a very keen observer of nature and possessed exceptional creativity. As a painter he created many deeply expressive pieces of art including the Mona Lisa. He spent his later years in the Vatican City, where he conducted many notable scientific experiments. A diagram of his "batlike" flying machine survives to this day. It is agreed that this machine could not have actually flown, but we can always speculate on what could have been ...

The eagle glided effortlessly against the blue summer sky. It floated almost magically as a warm updraft took it higher and higher. He waited patiently, spying it through his looking glass. Suddenly it flapped its wings and changed direction. Leonardo da Vinci observed every detail. His keen eyes saw the changes in the shape of the feathers, the expansion and contraction of every muscle, and how the bird shifted its weight in the sky.

Leonardo put down the looking glass and quickly picked up the drawing of his flying machine. He examined the drawing, and in his mind, he compared it to what he had just seen. A smile of satisfaction crossed his lips.

It will work, he thought.

He stared again at the parchment containing the drawing. It was complete other than it lacked a source of power. Leonardo's attempt to power the machine with foot pedals had been a failure that he deeply regretted. One of his assistants had broken a leg testing it and was left with a permanent limp.

Leonardo walked energetically across the Belvedere Court of Vatican City to his apartment. Although he was in his later years, Leonardo had the gait of a young man when he was enthusiastic about one of his projects. He was grateful that his patron, Pope Leo X, had provided him with accommodation at the Vatican as well as with an allowance. His mind was at peace, and he vowed to focus on his work as he did not know how many more years of life lay in his future. He always thought that life was too short, and that there was so much in the universe yet to discover.

His stride was broken as a familiar voice called out to him. He turned to see Michelangelo approaching. *He must be on his way to eat,* thought Leonardo. *He rarely takes a break from painting his frescoes.*

"Have you heard the news?" inquired Michelangelo.

"No."

"They have arrested Flavio and his wife. They say they are witches."

Leonardo and Michelangelo discussed the matter. Flavio was well known to both of them. He spent his time between Rome and the Tuscan countryside. Whereas Leonardo's field of study was mechanical sciences, Flavio focused on studying plants, and from them, he had created many potions and poultices. Both Leonardo and Michelangelo each knew of a few people whose illness was healed by Flavio's genius.

Neither knew Flavio's wife other than by sight, as her command of Italian was very poor. People were surprised when, years ago, Flavio returned from one of his trips with his new bride. Michelangelo told Leonardo that her name was Dreea and she came from Romania. Leonardo always thought she had a very striking look: exotically beautiful with jet-black, dead-straight hair, golden skin, and piercing green eyes.

"They are not witches, my friend," said Leonardo.

"I know, Leonardo, but these are dangerous times. There is news of heresy in the church in Germany, and the countryside is full of rumors of strange events. The Justice Council will decide their fate tonight. I will go to the trial to see what happens."

Leonardo went inside his apartment and had his evening meal in solitude. He had planned to walk into the countryside after his meal to inspect his flying machine. He changed his mind as he was disturbed at the thought of Flavio being on trial.

As usual Leonardo awoke early the next day. He maintained his solitude for the entire day, reading and taking notes. As the sun was setting, Michelangelo paid a visit.

"Leonardo, the council judged that they are guilty. They believe that Dreea is married to the devil and Flavio is under her spell. She was sentenced to death and he to the dungeons for life."

"You believe this, Michelangelo?"

"Of course not! But she looks so different from us, so exotic, and where does he get the knowledge to make his potions?"

"The punishment is too severe," continued Michelangelo. "Help me, Leonardo. The pope respects us and he is a good man. If we both go together, we can convince him to grace them with papal mercy and give them exile instead."

Leonardo agreed. "Yes, my friend, we must convince him. A life of exile and poverty is better than death and imprisonment."

After Michelangelo left, Leonardo sat for a long time in total darkness except for the light of the full moon streaming through the glass of his closed window. Once he collected his thoughts, he rose from his seat and quickly placed a manuscript and a small box into his pouch before purposefully walking out of the door. He walked through a narrow gate at the back of the Belvedere Court and into an open field. The moonlight created an ethereal blue landscape as he followed the uneven path toward a shed where his flying machine was concealed. It was a curious contraption made of wood and canvas. It had batlike wings and a cockpit just big enough for Leonardo.

The wheels of the machine creaked as Leonardo pushed it out of the shed. He climbed into the vehicle, removed the tiny box from his pouch, and riveted by enthusiasm connected it to wires attached to the cockpit's floor. As Leonardo pulled a lever, his ingenious contraption started to vibrate, not a crude mechanical vibration of the air, but a more subtle one. It was as if the device made the very fabric of space oscillate and made the machine and everything within it part of the air, not something apart from the air. He pulled more levers, and the wings gracefully flapped slowly. The machine lifted into the air gently, more like a butterfly than a bird.

That night, Leonardo laughed like a child as he glided over the Italian landscape. Sometimes he would flap the wings to change direction or height, but for most of the time there was silence as he drifted through the sky. His eyes became acclimated to the dim light of the moon. With a sense of awe he gazed at trees and houses and carts and people below, but he knew they could not see him unless he flew directly in front of the full moon.

Hours later, Leonardo softly alighted outside of the shed and, with a heavy heart, disconnected the box that had produced the power of flight. He climbed out of the cockpit and returned his contraption to its shed. On the long walk back to his apartment, he made a detour along a cliff overlooking the Tiber River.

How could I ever explain it? he thought, looking down at the river flowing swiftly hundreds of feet below him. *The entire design for the box that powers the machine came to me in a dream. I do not even fully understand how these vibrations work! They will say that I am a witch just like Flavio.*

From his pouch, he removed the box along with the manuscript. His eyes flooded with tears as he tossed the box over the cliff and watched it fall into the Tiber. He then opened the manuscript and examined it for one last time. On it was the elegant design of the amazing box that gave the power of flight to his machine. He stretched one arm over the cliff and released it, watching it slowly float down until it disappeared into the flowing river.

 Have you ever wondered why we count in dozens? Twelve seems to be such a completely arbitrary number to choose to count our eggs or our doughnuts. It is obvious to understand why we count in tens as we have ten fingers with which we can keep track of where we are in counting something. However, this is exactly why we count in dozens, it is just a lot harder to observe. The first person to observe it would have had sharp powers of observation like Leonardo looking at the eagle in the story. We count in dozens because one day some clever person observed that besides our thumbs, each of our fingers has three portions, three digits. By using the thumb of one hand to slide along the digits of the other four fingers of the same hand, that person realized that we could easily keep track of where we were in counting to twelve, and we only needed to use one hand to do it. If we use the other hand to keep track of how many twelves we have already counted, we could easily count to twelve groups of twelve or 144 and always keep track of where we are in the count. So by only using our fingers, if we count in tens, we can keep track of where we are up to ten. But if we count in twelves, we can keep track all the way up to 144! Therefore, counting in twelves is perhaps even more natural than counting in tens. We just have to be more observant to realize it.

This is not the only clever thing for which our fingers are useful. In the era before so much of our focus became dedicated to the screens of our phones and we stopped observing the world, another of our smart ancestors realized that you could use our hands to tell if we are approaching full moon or we are approaching new moon. If you can form the shape of the crescent of the moon that you observe in the night sky by curving the thumb and index finger of your right hand, it means that the moon is waxing so the nights are getting brighter, and if you can do it with your left hand, it means that the moon is waning or disappearing.

Notice that, in both instances, we have used the word *clever* or *smart*, words that are usually used synonymously with intelligence. What we specifically mean in these two cases is that someone is intelligent because they are able to use their power of observation to solve a practical problem.

Is this the conventionally accepted definition of intelligence used in business organizations today? I put forward that in most organizations it is not. In many organizations, significant operational problems persist that could be readily rectified through using the power of observation to derive practical solutions. Yet still these problems are allowed to persist usually due to the lack of empowerment of staff at the level where they can readily be fixed. The underlying cause of this lack of empowerment is that the organization does not value the observational intelligence of the staff at this level. In other words, the organization does not believe in or value observational intelligence in general. Lack of this observational intelligence is reflected in our language when people are accused of not having any common sense.

The wider point that I am making is that the definition of intelligence is not unique. This observational, practical intelligence is just one form. It is very different in nature from academic intelligence, the form of intelligence that has gained ascendancy in the corporate world. Rather than favoring observations, academic intelligence favors the application of paradigms that through careful academic research are meant to represent the real world. Those who practice academic intelligence have the tendency to solve problems by breaking them down into component parts, rather than solving the problem as a whole. This is reflected in our language when we say that someone does not understand the big picture.

Academic intelligence is, of course, very powerful. It provides structure to problem-solving, and it prevents the user from having to reinvent the wheel. Is it superior to observational intelligence? I do not believe that this is the correct question. The correct question is this: "Is it at all times better at solving a problem than observational intelligence?" The answer is clearly no, even if you believe that most of the time it is the most useful form of intelligence. It is unfortunate that many people treat this as a holy war. The application of one form of intelligence does not discredit the merits of the other forms. Magic is achieved when you know what form of intelligence to apply in a given situation. Doing otherwise is like a carpenter using a hammer to tighten a screw and using a screwdriver to drive a nail. This applies both at the corporate level and at the individual level.

There are many forms of intelligence other than observational and academic. Often when we think of artistic people we understand that they are creative but fail to realize that creativity is a form of intelligence. In fact, creativity is a very high form of intelligence. We have already spoken about intelligence based on observing the world and intelligence based on applying paradigms, but creativity is the sort of intelligence that is able to create something out of nothing. It is extremely powerful. It allows us to see things that do not yet exist and identifies a path to their creation. The gift of creativity is within everyone, but it's sometimes elusive, as it is developed through a process that is very different from standard academic learning. Creativity is much more than being able to paint, sculpt, or dance. At its heart it is about being able to see that which is yet to be. Lack of creativity manifests in corporate language when people are accused of lacking any vision.

Of course, there is also emotional intelligence, which has rightly gained a lot of prominence in the corporate world in recent years. The problem with cultivating emotional intelligence is understanding how it is assimilated. While it can be discussed in academic terms, it can only be understood through the application of one's inner humanity at an emotional level. This lack of understanding manifests in the corporate world when we see leaders doing other than what they preach. When leaders boast about being exceptional coaches, yet they emotionally destroy their staff it is a demonstration of totally misunderstanding emotional intelligence. I am always amazed at how such people are surprised when their teams eventually become underperformers or disintegrate.

There are other types of intelligence also. Intuition is certainly a high form of intelligence and I freely admit that there would also definitely be forms of intelligence of which I am unaware or do not understand. For example, it is a documented fact that August Kekulé discovered the ring-shaped molecular structure of the chemical benzene in a dream just as Leonardo "invented" the flight box in the story! I cannot even begin to describe that form of intelligence.

It is powerful to be aware of how wide and nuanced intelligence really is. I have observed that everyone is capable of developing all forms of intelligence. It only seems elusive when people do not realize that they need to use different methods for acquiring different forms of intelligence. Once a basic level of academic intelligence is assimilated, it is usually more productive to invest time in developing a toolbox of different forms of intelligence than doubling down on just one form. Too many people constantly pursue more and more academic qualifications and do not take the time to develop other forms of intelligence. Often it is this lack of balance in their intellect that acts as a barrier to progress up the corporate ladder.

Leonardo da Vinci is remembered as one of history's greatest genius because his intelligence was balanced and diverse. Apart from deep academic intelligence, he possessed amazing observational and creative intelligence. Possessing a balanced arsenal of differing types of intelligence creates the potential to become a powerful leader. To master anything someone must learn how to apply this intelligence—in all of its rich nuances.

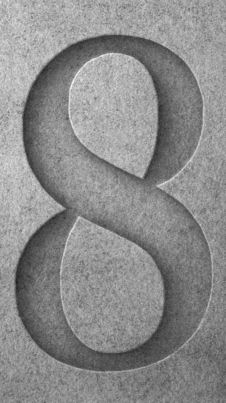

The Gemini Twins
Win a Battle

Know When to Win,
Know When to Lose

Castor and Pollux are divine twins in Greek and Roman mythology.
They are represented in the night sky by the constellation Gemini. In the
myths they are said to be divine healers. It has always amazed me that
ancient cultures in separate parts of the world have very similar beliefs.
This speaks to something deeply common among all of us humans.
For instance the ancient Indians, Irish, and Eastern Europeans all
believed in very similar characters: divine brothers that are healers. In
this story we imagine that the healer twins still operate among us ...

Heiani's thoughts and gaze ascended to the heavens above, illuminated by thousands of silvery stars set like tiny jewels against an inky blue background. This was her favorite time of the day, when after their evening meal, her father would lift and carry her to the seashore, gently leaning her against a tree so she could look at the sea and the stars. She was a happy child, but especially so at this time of the day being entranced by the sound of the waves, the salty air, and the glow of the stars. She never knew what it was like to have the use of her legs, but with the love of her family, she had adapted. However, at that time of the night, as her thoughts were in the sky, she would imagine herself running races against the other children from their fishing village.

A movement farther down the beach caught her eye. It was a moonless night, and the seashore would have been pitch black were it not for the dim yellow light from the kerosene lamp shining through the window of the kitchen of her humble wooden home. It was the old man. He had appeared in her village on a tiny Pacific island a week or so before, probably traveling on the steam ship that brought goods from the outside world from time to time. People on her island were not used to strangers, but his friendly manner gained him acceptance. Word soon spread that he was a master at repairing fishing nets and this made him even more welcome. He had spent that evening repairing her father's nets.

Returning her gaze to the stars, she was once again lost in thought.

"Those are Gemini, the twins."

Startled, she looked down to see the old man sitting on the beach near to her. Heiani was surprised that he had covered so much ground so quickly and silently. She watched curiously as he played with some pebbles that he had found in the sand. "Those stars you are looking at make the bodies of twin brothers."

"Are they both called Gemini?" asked Heiani.

"No, the stars are called Gemini. People from different nations of the world each know part of their story and called the brothers different names. The twins are Castor and Pollux according to the people from Greece. The Indians know them as the Asvins and the Irish call them the Divanno. They have many more names, too; your ancestors in these islands know them as Kane and Kanaloa.

"Do you know their story?"

Heiani shook her head to say no.

"Well, I will tell you the part the Greeks know ..."

Castor and Pollux were sons of the sky god Zeus. They were gifted with beauty, strength, and, above all, the art of healing. Being healers was the essence of their nature. It was the will of Zeus to make them extremely powerful, so even though they were the closest of friends as well as brothers, he encouraged them to spend their childhood in playful competitions of strength, speed, and wit. Castor had a furious desire to win and a hot temper. Pollux was the more curious and reflective of the two, with a thirst to explore new places. In everything, they were very evenly matched. The gods of Olympus would watch on at the splendor of their contests not knowing who would emerge the victor. As they matured into young men, they roamed the heavens and the mortal world on celestial horses. Their symbol all over the world became the crossed heads of two horses.

Once when their sister, the beautiful Helen, was kidnapped by Theseus, king of Attica, the twins set out to rescue her. As they approached Attica, they were ambushed by Theseus's huge army.

However, the sons of the sky god were more powerful than thousands of mortals. They proceeded to slay soldiers by the hundreds until suddenly, as night was falling, Pollux retreated. Seeing this, Castor followed his brother.

"Why did you spare them, brother? Victory was ours!"

"How can we win, Castor, with the blood of so many men on our hands?"

Pollux soothed Castor and convinced him that they must do their divine calling. As the sun rose the next morning, they stealthily entered the grim field of battle, but this time as healers not slayers. Magically, out of the rays of the rising sun, they created threads to sew the wounds of as many fallen soldiers as was within their power to save.

As they completed their task, Pollux said, "When we were approaching Attica, I saw a cave. Hide there until I return, brother. Victory will be ours yet."

"Victory should have been ours yesterday."

"Yesterday was not the time to win, not that way."

Castor did as Pollux asked. Days later he heard Pollux call out, "Come, brother! Now is the time to attack Attica."

Excited and curious he emerged from the cave to see Castor walking toward Attica carrying a white box encrusted with jewels of green. "I visited the enchantress Circe on the island of Aeaea," was all that he would say.

As they approached Attica, they could hear the clatter of armor as Theseus's army prepared to attack. Suddenly Pollux opened the box and an eerie silence descended. Castor grew confused and agitated.

"The magic of the sorceress, my brother," laughed Pollux, "all of the mortals of Attica have fallen into a deep sleep." As Theseus's entire army fell into a deep slumber, the brothers walked unchallenged into Attica and rescued their sister, who is known today as the legendary beauty, Helen of Troy.

The world has changed unimaginably since those days. Castor and Pollux still ride together through the celestial planets. Only occasionally do they now visit the world of mortals and when they do it is not together, Castor in search of contests and Pollux in search of exploration.

The old man ended his tale and saw that Heiani had fallen asleep.

In the morning when Heiani opened her eyes she was in her bed. It took a moment to realize her father must have carried her there after she fell asleep on the beach the previous night. He had done so many times before. As the first rays of light from the rising sun pierced through the window, Heiani was surprised by a rush of electricity in her body. She felt a pleasant tingle, as if the rays of sunlight were weaving their way through her legs like a silken thread. She realized with elation that this was the first time she had ever felt any sensation in her legs!

The old man! Was he ... Her thought dissolved as she sprang from her bed and ran for the first time in her life. She ran to the seashore to look for the old man. He was not there, and he was never to be seen on the island again. On the sand, she noticed the pebbles that he was playing with the night before. She picked them up and examined them. On the back of one was a pattern of two intertwined horse heads, formed as if burnt into the stone.

Thoughts of gratitude filled her heart and thoughts of winning a race against her friends filled her mind.

 For the second time in this book, I am going to refer to a British sitcom from the 1990s. Perhaps I have an unnatural fixation for them. This one is called *Black Adder*, and in one series, it featured a character called Queenie who was meant to be Queen Elizabeth I. She would argue the most ridiculous points of view, and when she came to the verge of losing the argument, she would always say, "Who's queen?" This statement came with the threat of a beheading if you disagreed. She had a pathological need to win every argument.

A desire to win is natural and it is reinforced by society. There is nothing wrong with it. The problem arises when the need to win becomes compulsive and emotional and overrides reason and logic as it did for Castor in the story. It is easy to fall into this trap of having a pathological need to win at all times and in every situation. This state of mind is very counterproductive, as winning always comes at a price. This is what Pollux understood. For him the price of going against his very nature was just too high.

Controlling the innate desire to win does not mean that you are mentally creating an excuse for failure; rather, this awareness prevents you from losing the battles that matter. We correctly glorify the acts of winning in sports. What we often overlook is that great coaches *manage* when their athlete or team wins. They understand that winning comes at the price of physical injury or fatigue. So they manage the situation in order that they are more likely to win when it matters and less likely when it does not matter. They shrug off irrelevant defeats because they see the bigger picture. High performance is obtained when resources are managed so that winning occurs almost every time *that it matters*. A key ingredient of success is developing the art of knowing when to win.

The bedrock of developing this art is understanding what winning means to you. I stress the words *to you*. Victory is personal, and a major trap in life is to allow others to define your sense of victory.

You have likely heard the analogy of running a marathon versus running a race about how to approach winning. The point of this analogy is that it is usually better to take the long-term perspective of a marathon, rather than the short-term perspective of a race. This is a very powerful point, as your time horizon is clearly relevant. It is important not to take an analogy too far though, as it is meant to illustrate one aspect of reality, not reality in totality.

We can build on our understanding of what winning means by considering another analogy: signal versus noise. Radio waves, especially in the early days of radio, do not in fact have the smooth fluctuating curves that we used to draw in science class. They have the same general curvy shape, but if you examine them closely, they are jagged. They look as if someone drew them while on a bumpy road.

The overall shape is called the *signal,* and the jaggedness is called the *noise.* It is the signal that transmits the music and voice over radio waves. The noise produces annoying static. A radio receiver needs to filter out the noise and only leave the signal. Life is like a radio wave. It has an overall trend or signal, but from day-to-day, it has a lot of ups and downs or noise. If winning for you is defined by the signal, as it almost always is, then you must learn to ignore or accept the noise.

Too often people lose money on the stock market because while they boast about using it to save for the long term, they react to day-to-day ups and downs. Too many businesses crumble or underperform because they waste resources and energy focusing on short-term profits and never make the investments and decisions necessary for long-term success. They react to the illusion of the noise and ignore the reality of the signal.

Of course, there are occasions when only the short term counts. If a tennis ball is about to hit your nose, the correct reaction is to duck, not to think about your next shot. These occasions are, however, the exception and not the rule. Most of the time winning at the game of life is about signal, not noise. You need to invest time in gaining a very clear understanding of what signal matters to you. Remember the point that victory is personal, therefore so too is your signal. You must ensure that you monitor that signal. However, if that signal does not change, you very rarely need to react no matter how much noise exists. You must always be acutely aware that the only way that the noise can affect the signal is if you allow it to cause you to make emotional decisions.

The innate desire to win can have an extremely detrimental effect on our lives if we allow it to shape how we approach negotiating with others. As we approach any negotiation, we need to be conscious of our innate desire to win. This innate desire can deceive us into believing that the best outcome of every negotiation is to win.

Often this is not the case because "winning" can come at the cost of damaging relationships or not building goodwill.

In a previous chapter, I have explained that the highest-yielding asset is goodwill, as goodwill constantly generates favorable treatment. A fair bit of the time, the value of that lost relationship or goodwill over the long term exceeds the rewards of "winning" the negotiation. It is important to develop the art of determining when "winning" is the less productive outcome. This is not always easy to achieve. When in doubt the best policy is to assume that the highest possible outcome of a negotiation is generating a situation where you have satisfying terms *and* both parties believe that they have won something. In fact, it is probably best to always operate in this fashion as things always average out over the long term. Negotiating in this manner is quick and very productive. On the other hand, negotiating in a selfish manner is tiring, tedious, and risks destroying valuable relationships for a few pennies.

The opposite side of the coin to winning is obviously losing. Everybody loses some of the time. A contest has no thrill unless there is the possibility of defeat, and no one can savor the sweetness of victory unless he or she has experienced the taste of defeat. However, it is important to understand how to make losing an asset.

First of all, it is important to realize that by definition a defeat is something that has already happened. It belongs to the past, not the present, and like everything of the past it is not real except to the extent that you make it real within your own head. Most people cannot resist their primal urge to kick others when they are down, even if it is with a feather-soft boot. This, however, can only affect someone if they are keeping the defeat alive within their head.

Thus, having dealt with losing at an emotional level, the next stage is to sow the seeds of winning within the manure of losing.

Losing is a precious gift holding within it an immense tome of information on how to win the next time. This gift is wasted unless the tome is studied. Having done all of this, you may still lose again as you may not yet have done enough things differently or you may simply be a victim of bad luck. God has a sense of humor. However, with the right consciousness, losing will be part of your noise and not change your signal.

It is also important to understand that on many occasions it is wise to consciously lose. There are occasions when it is better to take a small loss than to run the risk of a potentially large one. A very savvy person may deliberately take a small loss if winning did not matter much, and if by taking the small loss a valuable relationship can be created or deepened. That person sees the loss as a tremendous investment.

Kenny Rogers said it best in his song "The Gambler":

You got to know when to hold 'em,
Know when to fold 'em,
Know when to walk away,
Know when to run.

We can have a pathological urge to win all the time, but one of the ingredients of success is to master knowing when to win and when to lose.

Procrustes Makes
a Perfect Fit

| The Map Is Not the Territory |

In Greek mythology Procrustes was, among other things, an innkeeper and a master forger of metal. He had a curious ideal of perfection and endeavored to make the world fit to his ideal ...

Theseus cursed under his breath as an icy wind blew through his cloak and chilled him to his bones. He looked up at the bleak, gray sky then let his gaze fall to the lonely road ahead as it wound its way through the rocky, dun-colored landscape of the valley. Called the Sacred Way, he had followed this road from Athens toward the sacred site of Eleusis, although to him it looked more like the road to the gateway of hell than to anywhere sacred. To his right, Mount Korydallos towered like a giant fang emerging from the Netherworld.

He looked back, over his shoulder at the lonely inn and considered returning to spend the night. When he first saw the inn a few hours ago, its worn facade did not seem welcoming, and he considered bypassing it. With the sky darkening and fearing there may not be another inn for many miles, however, Theseus decided to visit the inn. He was happy that he chose to overlook its drab exterior. Inside the inn it was warm and comfortable, although decorated in a gaudy fashion with some of its walls glaring back at him in a kaleidoscope of color. He was pleased to discover that the owner and innkeeper was Procrustes, famous all over Greece as a master metalworker. It was also known that, perhaps because he was such a creative genius, he was eccentric. Apart from the lurid decoration on the interior, Theseus perceived this eccentricity in the way that Procrustes looked at someone sideways when he spoke and in the elongation of his words as he spoke in a somewhat shrill voice.

However, his eccentricity was more than recompensed by his warm manner and hospitality. In the company of one other guest, a young man from a village near Eleusis, Theseus enjoyed a delicious meal washed down with an abundance of fine mead. The young man introduced himself as Vlassis and told Theseus that he had arrived earlier that day on his way to Athens and found the inn so comfortable that he decided to spend the night.

As the two men relaxed after their meal, Procrustes entertained them with amusing stories of some of the previous visitors to the inn. As the atmosphere became more convivial, he opened a cabinet to show them some of his best works as a master metalworker: intricately engraved hammers and saws and some of the finest swords and daggers that Theseus had ever seen. Noticing that Vlassis had dozed off in his weariness, Procrustes invited Theseus to follow him to another room, which he promised contained the pinnacle of his work.

As he followed Procrustes through an elaborate doorway, Theseus laid his eyes on the most beautiful bed he had ever seen. It was a sight to behold for anyone, with ornate carvings and exquisite craftsmanship. Procrustes confided in a soft voice that the bed was magical, that any traveler that lay on the bed would find the bed to be the perfect fit and would become as perfect as the bed.

"I was going to give the bed to Vlassis for the night, but I can see, sir, that you are a man of character. You should rest on it tonight," enticed Procrustes.

Though he felt unusually tired and Procrustes was very persistent, Theseus decided that he needed to make haste as he was on an important mission for the king of Athens. Lives depended on his speed. Out of a sense of duty, he left the inn.

As the frigid wind bit into his bones and the bleak environment oppressed his senses, he considered returning to the inn to spend the night on that beautiful bed. As a skilled warrior though, the force of his will was strong. He looked at the daunting road ahead and marched onward, thinking that at least young Vlassis would get to enjoy the wonderful bed.

No more people must perish, thought Theseus. Like the king, he was disturbed that too many travelers on the road to Eleusis were never seen again. There were tales of a monster roaming this bleak valley devouring travelers. His mission from the king was to slay the monster so that citizens of Athens could again travel the road safely.

After a few hours' trek along the dismal road, he was approached by a rider on a trotting horse. Both the rider and horse appeared to be haggard; Theseus could see the man perspiring from his journey, even in the cold air. Through his gasps the rider inquired, "Sir, have you seen a lad along the way? He is my son Vlassis."

Surprised, Theseus replied, "I know him. We had a fine lunch at the inn of Procrustes. Do not worry. He is safe."

"Come with me, please. We must get to the inn before my son takes rest!"

"Sir, you can go along to speak to your son at the inn. I must continue on my way. I am on a mission from the king to slay the monster that hunts in this valley," Theseus said, turning away from the man to continue his journey.

"But Procrustes *is* the monster!"

Theseus stopped and stared at the rider in complete shock and amazement.

The rider told him that everyone in his village also thought that a beast prowled the valley eating travelers—at least they did until a gaunt, crippled beggar wandered through their village half-mad. He was unusually tall and could barely walk; it was as if his bones were not fully connected to his joints.

A villager recognized him, though mutilated, as her husband Ermis who disappeared on the way to Athens almost a year before. Her patience and care for Ermis lessened his incoherence and he managed to explain what happened to him. He had stopped to rest at Procrustes's inn and had a wonderful meal and lots of mead. As he lay asleep on the beautiful bed, the same bed that had been offered to Theseus just hours before, Ermis awoke in incredible pain, finding that his limbs were fastened to the corners of the bed by chains. Procrustes stood over him, turning a wheel above the bed that Ermis hadn't noticed before. In insane delirium Procrustes told Ermis the bed was crafted to be of a specific length, a length that he believed to be the perfect fit for any traveler who lay upon it. Procrustes was stretching Ermis, pulling his limbs away from his body to meet the proportions of the bed.

Ermis screamed as Procrustes turned a wheel to stretch his limbs. Through his screams Ermis could hear Procrustes explain coldly, "It is my duty to make my guests as perfect as the bed. If they are too tall for the bed, I must use my hammers, saws, and swords to shorten their limbs until they fit to the bed. But if they are too short, like you, I must stretch them using ropes and pulleys."

Ermis managed to survive the pain of his ordeal, but it left him broken and driven mad. Procrustes left him in the forest to die of his wounds and be eaten by animals. He could not recall the next year of his life until his wife nursed some sanity back into him. He believed that by the grace of Zeus he recovered from his wounds and roamed the wildness as a mad beggar in that year before he managed to wander home.

On hearing the story of Ermis, Theseus joined the rider and the two hastened to the inn arriving just as Vlassis was about to retire to bed. To the relief of the rider, his son had not yet endured the tortures of the bed of Procrustes. Theseus's skill at combat was far superior to that of Procrustes, who was quickly injured and subdued. The men tied Procrustes to his "perfect" bed while they searched the inn. To their horror, they discovered the belongings of many lost travelers. A few weeks later, on the orders of the king, Procrustes was given a taste of his own cruel medicine. Justice was served, and Procrustes met his end at the hands of the very act he had inflicted on others.

No one knows for certain what was mankind's first tool. Perhaps it was a club, or fire, or clothes made of animal skin. However, an equally likely candidate is a map—not one as we know it today, but rather a simple diagram drawn with a twig on the sandy ground used by someone to explain to others where they should go to hunt. It is natural for human beings to use drawings to represent the world around us. They aid in communication and allow us to simplify something that is naturally very complicated and interrelated. As society advanced so too did the complexity of these maps. By "map" I refer to any model that man

has created to represent the world. Apart from traditional maps, these include business models, models of human behavior, and any mental idea that we carry in our head to represent the world around us.

A problem has arisen over time, though. We often forget that our maps, as powerful as they may be, are not the real world. They only represent the real world and do so only partially. The map is not the territory. We have developed a tendency to have such faith in our maps that we believe that our maps are the real world. Procrustes's mental image, or map, was his ideal bed. If someone could not conform to his ideal bed, then he believed that they were not perfect and "adjusted" them rather than discard his ideal and offer them a different bed. If we deeply reflect we will notice that a tendency has developed in mankind to fight reality, to hold on to our mental images even when they no longer reflect reality, to even try to change reality to make them conform to our mental maps.

A friend of mine was in an eerie situation where he was told that he could not sit on an empty chair because someone else was already sitting on that chair at that very moment! The person giving him the instruction imagined that the chair was currently occupied and wanted my friend to comply with her imagination. The person giving the instruction was, of course, unfortunately suffering from a mental illness. More specifically, that person saw reality not as it was but as she was imagining it to be and expected everyone else to conform accordingly.

We may find such a situation a little bit amusing, but the sad reality is that analogous situations happen all of the time in the corporate world. You do not have to look hard in the business world to find people who have predefined notions of how a business operates, how a business is performing, or who define problems in a way so as to match a solution that they have already created. They try to impose their notions or solutions on the business without bothering to examine the actual business landscape. While any rational person would agree that theories should be formed from observations, these people only observe things that fit the theories that they already have. Often, as consultants, they are paid a tidy sum by the corporate world for proffering such dubious advice.

There is a disconnect between reality and the maps that they carry in their heads. They simply do not understand that a map will never be the same as the territory. This approach almost always fails, to the detriment of their career and to the detriment of the business. People going through their careers need to understand that they look so much smarter and so much more useful not when they quote technical academic material, but when they demonstrate that they understand the real world around them.

Failure from the disconnect between reality and our mental "maps" is visible in the commercial world all of the time. Marketing executives often develop products that suit their own ideal for the product rather than one their customers want, and when these products fail blame it on the customer's unsophisticated taste. Entire businesses fail because their leadership stubbornly holds on to a mental image of how their industry is meant to operate. In holding on to this mental image, they fail to see that the world is changing around them as when photography moved from film to digital or movie rentals moved from DVDs to streaming.

At the time of this writing, I am in my early fifties, and it is truly amazing how much the world has changed over the thirty years of my working life. When I attended university in London in the years straddling the end of the 1980s and the beginning of the 1990s, personal computers were things found in computer labs. It would be extremely rare for anyone to possess one in their dorm room or at their home. By the time I left university and started to work full time in 1992, there was still not a computer on every desk. The pervasiveness of personal computers was, however, exponentially increasing. Within a year there was a computer on every desk and within a few years emails were the preferred means of communication. This was the dawn of a new era, not so much because technology advanced, but rather because this technology changed how we collectively think. The advancement in technology allowed the creation of much more powerful models of reality or "maps." While the development of these models was positive, it also dramatically deepened the problem of believing that the "map" was the territory.

Early in my career one of my bosses used to call me "half and half." He called me this because I spent the first year or two of my working career in the dying stages of a previous era of doing business. Like him I understood how to make decisions with limited computing power and fewer preconceived mental models. However, I also understood how to function in the new era of decision-making aided by technology like computerized business models and databases. Unlike me, while he totally understood the old mindset, his thought pattern was not native to the new mindset. He called me "half and half" because I was comfortable with both ways of thinking.

I believe that we have made great progress in how business is conducted over my thirty-year career. However, I also believe that a number of positive aspects of the "old era" have been lost, mainly having to do with being able to function with less reliance on our maps.

When I first started to work, my job was to do calculations for life insurance companies. To make a decision about a single life insurance policy involves hundreds of pieces of arithmetic. Multiply this by at least a couple of hundred thousand policies for even a small life insurance company, and the enormity of the calculations becomes apparent. Prior to the 1990s, this had to be done with little computing power. Relying on computerized models was not even an option.

The World War Two generation were masters of operating in this environment. I had the pleasure of working with a few experts from this era. They were a different breed. They possessed a different form of intelligence. They thought differently. Their environment allowed them to think more freely as they had no computing power to rely upon. They approached every problem by giving it as much thought as it warranted in a relaxed fashion. They would figure out how accurate their calculations needed to be and do just enough calculations for the level of accuracy required. They understood the big picture so well that they would often be able to do all of their calculations on a small piece of paper, sometimes literally the back of a napkin. They understood that while their output was not 100 percent accurate, it was accurate enough for the purpose.

This approach more or less reflects how all decisions were made until the early 1990s, in a world where there were limited computers to crunch masses of numbers. There was no internet to research how everyone else did something, so people needed to be self-reliant and creative.

There are three items that have been deemphasized since that era that would be extremely useful to anyone. The first is that there used to be an emphasis on individually tailored solutions versus trying to fit every problem to a set of predetermined solutions. Procrustes had only one solution for a perfect night's sleep: his perfect bed. He tried to solve the problem of each of his guests by making them fit to his one bed. Many times in the business world, solutions are in fact "beds of Procrustes." This is why the term "bed of Procrustes" is sometimes used in business jargon. We love the solution so much that we try to bend or cut the problem so that the solution will work even though it may not solve the real problem or may even create greater problems. Secondly, there used to be more of a reliance on the skill of making decisions at an individual level rather than collective decision-making. There was more self-responsibility. The third is there used to be an emphasis on the usefulness of a solution rather than its precision. Anyone who can master these three skills will have a significant advantage in their career.

The point about favoring usefulness as opposed to accuracy is very important. Anyone in any career is heavily rewarded for being able to make quality decisions and being able to make them quickly. Too often people avoid making a decision by collecting more and more information on which to make the decision, to the point where they mentally drown in all of the information that they have collected. In the face of their self-inflicted information overload, they freeze. It is critical to avoid this trap and develop the art of knowing the minimum amount of information needed to make a useful decision. In other words, learn to find the correct balance between precision and usefulness.

To be clear, I am not arguing that the thought processes from the previous era were superior. All I am saying is that they were different. Clearly pervasive technology in the business world has been of tremendous benefit. However, I believe that some important lessons from the past era have been discarded to the detriment of the careers of many people. We can give ourselves a distinct advantage if we carry forward useful approaches from the past and modify them for the current environment.

10

Arachne's
Flawed Web

The Virtues of Delegating
Tasks and Retaining Blame

The scientific name for a spider is an arachnid. This name alludes to a Greek myth in which Arachne was turned into a spider by the goddess Athena as punishment for her arrogance. The following story is not the traditional version of that myth as told by the Greek poet Ovid. However, perhaps this version sheds an insightful light on Arachne's character and why she was punished ...

A rachne was the first spider. But before she was a spider, she was a woman with a gift for weaving.

One day Cora, an old skilled village weaver, saw a little girl walking outside of her shop in a worn, dusty dress. She instantly took a liking to the child. "Come inside, child. I will weave you a dress," said the old lady. Cora noticed the child's fascination with the craft of weaving and kindly made Arachne her apprentice. Arachne had a natural talent for weaving and an insatiable appetite to learn. She quickly absorbed everything that Cora taught her.

Soon Arachne's skill at weaving surpassed that of her teacher. She was a true prodigy, and by the time that she was a young woman, she was famous all over Greece for her ability to create incredible weavings of such quality that they seemed ethereal. She moved from her village to Athens and established a store for her pieces of work that attracted a lofty clientele. Out of affection for Arachne, Cora, who was very old at the time, chose to also leave the village and work for Arachne at the store.

They were working in the shop together when Arachne noticed a customer examining her merchandise. She was an unusually tall woman, her hair covered with a purple scarf that draped over her shoulders to overlap with her fine, ivory-white dress. On examining an intricately woven dress, the customer noticed a flaw in the embroidery and pointed this out to Arachne. Arachne had woven that dress personally, but she replied that it was the old lady's fault, as she was losing her eyesight.

The customer commented that despite this one flaw the dress was so magnificent that it seemed heavenly. She mentioned that Arachne must have been truly blessed by Athena, the goddess of craft and weaving.

"My talent is my own, not a gift from a goddess," Arachne replied curtly. She boldly stated that her work was so great that even the goddess Athena would be honored to wear one of her dresses.

The customer lowered her scarf to reveal glowing red hair. Her green eyes sparkled as she grew even taller to tower over everyone in the store. She revealed herself to be the goddess Athena. Everyone in the store bowed down immediately, even Cora with her ancient joints. Only Arachne remained standing. Athena was annoyed by Arachne's arrogance but maintained a calm demeanor. She decided to further test Arachne's character. She told Arachne that she would return the following morning and would be more than happy to wear a dress woven by her if the weaving was intricate and perfect.

Arachne was elated. She imagined how her fame would grow and the social power she would wield if Athena wore her dress. She chased all the customers out of the store and locked the door so she could work on the weaving until the following morning. Cora advised Arachne that the time was very short to weave such a dress so they should split the work between them. Arachne was fearful that she might have to share the credit with the old lady, so she insisted on doing all of the work herself. She angrily accused Cora of doubting her abilities and told her to leave until the next morning.

When Cora returned at sunrise, a tired Arachne was holding a beautiful woven dress. Looking at it closely though, Cora could see that while it was beautiful, it was not perfect. In some places she could see flaws in the embroidery, errors that Arachne clearly had made in haste. She also noticed that the sleeves and hem of the dress were not intricate enough for a goddess. Clearly, Arachne ran out of time to make the dress as intricate as it could have been. The old lady pointed out these flaws and pleaded to Arachne to beg the goddess for understanding that the time was too short to create a perfect dress. Cora's advice stoked the fire of Arachne's rage. She accused her of malicious jealousy and harshly told Cora to leave the store and never return.

As Cora tearfully turned to leave, Athena arrived. With her divine eyes, she had observed all that had happened since her conversation with Arachne the previous day. Angered by her arrogance and her treatment of the old lady, Athena transformed Arachne into a spider so that as a solitary, unloved creature she may forever weave her web with neither fame nor glory.

Every society has fables and myths, such as the myth of Arachne, concerning the downfall of people who fall in love with power and fame and who consequently manifest arrogance, greed, and self-praise. Perhaps these stories are so globally prevalent because they speak of a universal truth about our dark side. Deep down we all know that power tends to corrupt even those who originally had pure intentions.

These myths also reveal an unspoken and disturbing awareness that people of poor character have a hunger for fame and power over others and unless we are vigilant, they will become our overlords to our detriment. It is interesting that such stories follow a pattern in which someone's lust for power is initially successful but eventually greed or arrogance causes their downfall. Perhaps this reflects not just moral wishful thinking but also an awareness that a leader succumbing to the ill effects of fame and power will eventually be destroyed by the inevitable consequences of his or her own behavior. In addition, these stories convey a universal truth that nature tends to cleanse herself of such leaders. They are unceremoniously removed or their reputation sullied, making them powerless, though this is often after they inflict significant pain and suffering on others.

As we aspire for leadership, we need to be on guard against being corrupted by power. To do so we need to begin by understanding the duties and responsibilities of a leader. Leadership comes with many benefits. It provides salaries and bonuses well above that of the average worker. It conveys prestige and some degree of fame. It offers a platform for a leader to create his or her vision, shaping organizations and perhaps even influencing entire societies. It allows leaders to have their voices heard. Unfortunately, many who achieve significant positions of leadership see leadership as a destination and proceed to enjoy its trappings oblivious to the other side of the coin. Simply put, they ignore their duties as a leader.

The objective of this book is to offer guidance on the softer skills of success, the lack of which often impedes someone's progress in the corporate world in particular, but also in life in general. My hope is that these simple insights will not only assist people in achieving their full potential but also encourage them to pursue their dreams in a fashion that creates less suffering for others. It is within this context that I address the matter of the necessity for every leader to operate with a sense of personal duty. The more significant issue is not the inevitable poor results from bad leadership but rather the significant damage that occurs at a human level. This damage is both to the leader and to the team being led and can be so easily avoided once the leader has a sense of service and a sense of humility.

It is not the actions of leaders that define their duty but rather the mindset with which they do these actions. For a leader to be successful over the long term the actions of that leader must be performed with a sense of personal responsibility and service and not out of the joy of exercising power.

It should be obvious that the fundamental use of a leader is to take control of an organization, place, or situation. The term "control" is implicit within the term "leader." If leaders do not take personal responsibility for everything under their charge, what they are subconsciously doing is saying they are not in control. This lack of control should attack the very core of everyone who sees themselves as a leader because it should challenge their self-identity. It is also obvious that if someone is in control, then he or she must be the ultimate cause for things going well or things going badly. A leader is the interface between the people they lead and the outside world. Therefore, as far as the outside world is concerned, good leaders should accept blame for everything that goes wrong in the team they lead whether or not it is personally their fault. They are in control; therefore, they are to blame. Of course, within the team, screened from the outside world, the leader must also coach the person that was actually responsible for the fault so that their team becomes stronger.

Once anyone takes personal responsibility for anything, it creates the frame of mind where they seek to find a solution to what went wrong or can go wrong. When someone does not take personal responsibility, they tend to leave the discovery of this solution to others, which is really no different from leaving it to chance. This is exactly why leaders who have the mindset of accepting personal responsibility (and hence personal blame) are much more effective than leaders who do not.

Pay attention to the language of various leaders and you will notice this point. At a national level, inept politicians blame other countries, their own citizens, or other political parties for their failings. At a corporate level, inept leaders blame the economy and their staff. However good leaders do not waste time passing on the blame. They talk about what they are doing, and if pressed, they will admit that they could have done more in the past. Apart from noticing that leaders who accept blame are much more successful, you would also notice that leaders who pass on blame tend to be ridiculed in their absence.

The acceptance of blame is an extremely powerful tonic for a leader. It does not undermine leaders, but rather it strengthens them. At a human level, such leaders gain the respect of their subordinates, their superiors, and people outside of their organization. It shows strength of character. Acceptance of blame provides the catalyst and the adrenaline to find effective solutions efficiently and rapidly.

There is, however, a danger to this mindset that needs to be avoided. That is the tendency to micromanage, even though many micromanagers still pass on blame to others. However, micromanagement will be avoided once one remembers that another key duty of a leader is to delegate—something that Arachne refused to do, because she wanted to take singular credit for success.

As for control, clearly the concept of "leading others" is implicit in the term *leader*. Any rational person would understand that the whole point of having a team is to try to use every member of the team to their fullest potential and to try to achieve a situation where the team in totality is stronger than the sum of each individual member. Unlike Arachne, leaders who understand this have the confidence to delegate. A powerful leader is effective at delegating each task to the most appropriate team member.

Good leaders have the humility to understand that success is achieved when most members of their teams are better than they are at most things. They have such confidence in their own leadership that they constantly seek to add team members who are better than they are in many aspects. They do not pack their team with weak people just to make themselves look strong. They also grow the strength of people who are already in their teams.

Often leaders claim that they develop their staff, but the acid test is whether they accept blame for the shortcomings of their team or whether they pass on the blame to the very staff that they claim to nurture. Organically, every creature follows a leader because, apart from providing a sense of direction, a leader provides a sense of safety. The leader/follower relationship in most organizations, however, is not determined organically in that when people enter an organization the leader is already determined so they follow them as a requirement and not necessarily as a conscious choice. This is why leaders must make the effort to earn the trust and respect of each new team member. The need for a sense of safety requires that a good leader fosters an environment where people feel safe. This is achieved when people feel they are treated fairly and are not blamed unduly. Apart from this sense of safety being something that everyone deserves, a team operating in such an environment is naturally extremely powerful. The sense of safety fosters innovation and high performance. Such a sense of safety is destroyed by poor leaders who constantly throw their staff under the proverbial bus as happened to Cora in the story. Trust as an aspect of leadership is so critical that it is developed fully in chapter 12, in which Julius Caesar burns the bridge over the Rubicon River to prevent his troops from retreating.

The acceptance of blame by a leader is a heavy burden to bear and takes a huge mental toll on leaders. It is the flip side of the coin to all the fine trappings that come with being a leader. Anyone aspiring to leadership must prepare for this aspect of leadership. To bear this burden a leader must find a way to develop significant mental strength. The process of this development is personal, so it is specific to every person. In deriving a personal approach, it is important to understand that no one can bear the burden of leadership all the time just as someone cannot carry a heavy weight constantly. Every leader needs to find a means to take a break from their duties in order to recharge and achieve a sense of balance.

11

Sacagawea
Makes It Happen

| The Gift of Realizing There Are Many
| Things That Money Can Never Buy |

It is agreed by many historians that the success of the Lewis and Clark expedition would have been in serious doubt were it not for the presence and goodwill of Sacagawea, who started the expedition as the humblest member of the team. This is part of her story ...

The sound of their hooves was not thunderous at first, but she was easy to wake these days. This, she knew, was a band of raiders moving swiftly on horseback toward her village. Her tribe, the Lemhi Shoshone, had enjoyed relative peace for generations in this northwestern corner of the Rocky Mountains. That is, until her people's rivals had begun to barter furs, skins, and food for muskets and ammunition in recent years. She was twelve when the Hidatsa marauders took her that night. The status of the daughter of a revered chief, sister of rising warrior Cameahwait, could not help her; it only made her more valuable to trade.

One year later her captors sold the girl to a craggy man nearly three decades her senior, looking for a second wife to aid his other Shoshone bride, Otter Woman. Toussaint Charbonneau was a French-Canadian trapper from Quebec, a man adapted to the harsh and often morally absent terrain of the developing Western frontier. Wanting a wife, he traded pelts and meat to the Hidatsa for the girl. They called her Sacagawea. "What's your name?" Charbonneau asked her in Shoshone, proficient enough in the language himself. "I am Bird Woman," she replied.

Sacagawea's spirit had long danced in harmony with the rugged wilderness that surrounded her, but now, kidnapped and forced into a world unknown, Sacagawea found herself shackled by new chains. Charbonneau, a hardened and foul man, tried to bend, twist, and beat her unwavering resolve to his rule. Yet within the depths of her torment, Sacagawea clung fiercely to the remnants of her spirit. She understood who she was and would always be. Her courage burned with an unyielding flame, a light that flickered in defiance of the darkness that now engulfed her. She knew that her survival depended on her ability to adapt, to navigate a treacherous world with an unwavering gaze.

It was in this time of despair that a fateful encounter breathed life into the embers of her existence.

The Corps of Discovery, a US Army unit charged with exploring the newly acquired lands of the Louisiana Purchase and beyond, reached Charbonneau and Sacagawea's North Dakota homestead near the last weeks of fall in 1804. Knowing that their journey would require a translator competent in Western indigenous languages, the party was pleased to learn of a French-speaking frontiersman married to two Shoshone young women who may be willing to help their dangerous mission. When the party arrived, the calls of exploration and money echoed through Charbonneau's ears. The chance to return to her family and ancestral homeland spoke even louder to Sacagawea, drawing her to the side of Meriwether Lewis and William Clark, leaders of the Corps of Discovery.

Sacagawea, with scars etched upon her body and the echoes of torment still fresh in her heart, faced a choice. In truth, it was not much of a choice at all, for a native woman of her time knew that her agency was a fleeting illusion. And yet, with her eyes locked on the horizon, she saw a glimmer of possibility—a chance to shape her destiny, if only in a small way.

"Will you guide us?" Lewis asked Charbonneau, his voice tempered by both curiosity and want. Charbonneau, turning to Sacagawea, relayed the request, knowing they would need her languages and knowledge of the land ahead of them. Sacagawea met the men's stares. "I will guide them," she told Charbonneau.

Her words carried a hidden message—a silent reminder that she was more than a captive, more than a slave. She was a woman whose worth extended far beyond the conditions that bound her. And so, with little more than a nod, the explorers thanked her.

Sacagawea was pregnant, however, and she would be giving birth in a matter of weeks. Lewis and Clark decided to build Fort Mandan, a small military bastion made of timber along the Missouri River in modern-day North Dakota. The expedition would winter there and await the birth of Charbonneau and Sacagawea's son, Jean Baptiste, or "Pompy" as Clark would affectionately call him. In April, with Pompy just shy of his second month in the world, the expedition departed Fort Mandan heading north on the Missouri. The crew of roughly forty-five packed into small boats known as pirogues, muscling themselves upriver using long poles to dig into the riverbed and propel each of the watercraft against the current.

When Charbonneau accidently tipped over their pirogue, Clark wrote that he watched in horror from the riverbank as nearly every journal and record of the expedition plunked into the water. The loss of all these records would have been devastating. Then, to his amazement, he witnessed Sacagawea dive into the water and rescue the crates, risking her life to swim with them across the currents to the shore. No one had realized that she was a strong enough swimmer to save the journals, so none would have been the wiser if she stayed onshore and looked on in apparent helplessness. Clark was humbled by her selfless act, neither done for money nor out of fear of brutality from Charbonneau. Her act of pure goodwill deepened his respect of her.

"Squaw, I know you do not understand my words, but thank you," Clark told her. "You have just saved every record of our being here, and of our findings for every place we have journeyed across to be here. You have just delivered proof of the enterprise's very existence." Sacagawea returned a knowing nod, her eyes firm but calm.

Like a falcon soaring against the wind, Sacagawea became the pillar upon which the expedition leaned. Her presence, a beacon of determination and know-how, buoyed the group's quest through the perilous unknown. Her knowledge of the land, a compass of survival in an unforgiving terrain, carried them onward. She knew within her soul that she had to lead this lost party, men she considered less harmful than the many others to which she had grown tragically accustomed. This journey, and her place at the bow of it, affirmed her dignity and rightful offerings of respect and esteem from any man or woman. It offered the chance to prove that she was meant to be more than a slave, more than a forced bride and servant. She was Sacagawea, daughter of Chief Smoked Lodge, sister of Cameahwait, great hunters and warriors. She was born to lead and aid those in need. And ultimately it would be her fate.

It was her generosity that set her apart. In her interactions with both the known and unknown, Sacagawea extended her hand, bridging divides with an innate understanding of humanity's shared struggles. Her kindness, a balm to both weary and wary souls, weaved a tapestry of unity amid the vast expanse.

When the group required horses to cross the forbidding Rocky Mountains, Lewis and Clark again turned to Sacagawea. "We cannot cross on foot," Lewis told François Labiche, the party's French-Canadian-Omaha private who served as a conduit between English, French, and Algonquin speakers.

Labiche explained the dilemma to Charbonneau, who in turn explained it to Sacagawea. With little more than a nod, Sacagawea pointed west toward the mountains, where the group traveled to a headwater from which smoke could be seen streaming into the skies above them. Sacagawea made her way to the camp.

"Brother ... it is you!"

Lewis and Clark watched from the shoreline as Sacagawea ran to the chief, a strong and commanding man. The two embraced and conversed in a language neither Lewis nor Clark could understand. Soon the village had gathered, and the soldiers served as audience to the reunion of Sacagawea and Cameahwait, her brother.

The chief gave them horses and all the food and supplies his tribe could afford to carry the expedition over the mountains. Sacagawea knew they would not survive if they did not move quickly and without any costly mistakes. She guided them through invaluable gaps known today as Gibbons Pass and Bozeman Pass, delivering the corps over the formidable mountain range and on to the western-most coastline of the American Pacific.

And as they reached the final frontier, where the endless expanse of the Pacific Ocean stretched before them, Sacagawea stood at the precipice of her own liberation. The wind whipped through her long raven hair, carrying with it the echoes of a life redeemed. She had ventured beyond the confines of her captivity, and in doing so she had discovered some measure of freedom herself.

Sacagawea navigated the intricacies of language, her voice a vessel of understanding, enabling communication between cultures. Her and Pompy's presence helped to disarm any conflicts before they could ignite, serving as a token of peace and a symbol of friendly intentions. As the expedition reached its culmination, Sacagawea's journey continued, etching her story into the annals of history.

Though her footsteps may have faded into the sands of time, her spirit lives on in the hearts of those who dare to dream and persist against all odds. Her name, now synonymous with adventure, continues to inspire generations who dare to dream, explore, and cherish the bonds that make us human. Her story is a reminder that in the face of adversity true strength lies not only in personal resolve but also in the profound connections forged through understanding, duty, and compassion.

 I am sure that most of us will recall those old movies where the Greek gods of Mount Olympus would look down to see the activities of mortals like us. The gods would entertain themselves by looking down at our activities, the activities of their creations, with a good deal of detachment. They were never bored of this activity as they created an endless source of entertainment with so many diverse types of people engaging in so many different activities. They could look down at the farmers, the fisherman, the politicians, the prostitutes, and the priests, to name a few. The variety of entertainment would be amazing as each group had their distinct daily routine, conversations, challenges, and triumphs. The entertainment of the gods was indeed wonderful. What an amazing creation they made!

Above the rich and powerful, the kings and rich merchants, they would, however, be most proud that they created people like Sacagawea, people who may be of humble backgrounds but were rich in character and selflessness.

It is interesting to consider what the gods would see from their lofty view. They would notice that each group had a singular focus on their own activities and challenges. For each group the most important activities and challenges in the world were their own. They would also notice that because members of each group had so much in common, they could easily babble on to each other about whatever it was they did. It would be apparent to the gods that, in a sense, each group lived within their own world. The gods would also view the ongoings in the towns and cities where members from the different groups would have to interact. They would notice that even in these places, there is a great deal of cliquishness as people are naturally more comfortable with others who have the same challenges, culture, and jargon.

The gods would have taken joy in the diversity of their creation. In their wisdom, they would understand how important the activity of each group was for the overall well-being of mankind. They would watch as leaders who shared this understanding emerged and inspired different groups of people to cooperate with each other to form civilizations.

As different groups of people started to interact more and more, they would notice how cumbersome it was, before money was invented, for people that produced different things to trade with each other. The gods would have been delighted when man invented money to use as a store of value and a common form of tender to replace bartering and in the process make everyone's life so much easier. The gods though would have perhaps been concerned as mankind became more and more fixated with money especially when people developed a tendency to use money as the main measure of success. However, they would have taken some solace in the fact that not everyone fell into this trap, at least not all of the time, and so many of their creations still did not define success mainly in terms of money. Like Sacagawea, many of their creation chose to act not out of reward but out of goodwill.

It is interesting that some things never change. In ancient times everyone's sphere of experience was small, which caused fishermen to see the world through the lens of what they did, the same with farmers and all other trades. Even though today our sphere of experience is relatively massive, we still fall into the trap of seeing the world through our own eyes and our own values, and forgetting that our perspective and values do not encompass the full range of perspectives and values of everyone. This is especially the case with people who default to money as a measure of success, they too often discount the fact that their world of pursuing the creation of wealth is not the whole world.

It is an undeniable fact that as someone progresses in management, they become more and more focused on financial targets and less and less on doing a particular activity. This becomes very pronounced when someone becomes a member of the senior executive of an organization. There is nothing inherently wrong with this as long as the focus on wealth creation does not create tunnel vision and cause someone to ignore the fact that there are many more drivers, other than the accumulation of wealth, to human motivation. Of course, money is important to everyone. But does money drive everyone? The answer is no, not all of the time and not uniquely. The ability to lead people is core to success in management so this sort of tunnel vision is extremely counterproductive, as it impedes someone's ability to form and lead teams.

Clearly everyone tries to find a job that they enjoy. This makes life more fulfilling. However, in many cases this is not achieved. In many other cases even when people do a job that they enjoy, there is something else that they enjoy even more and would prefer to be doing. In a very real sense people are in these jobs just for the money. The tendency in the corporate world is to view this as a bad thing, so many people pretend to be in love with their job while in their heart they are not. The reality is that people have always been and will always be created with a myriad of different interests. A significant portion of people, perhaps even the majority, will be more interested in something other than their career whether that other thing is playing the guitar, cycling across the country, or raising a family. Is anything wrong with this? Of course not. Look again at the world from the perspective of the gods of Olympus. Human beings have a great diversity of interests. The moneymakers are only one type of human being. It is this diversity that makes us strong and makes us interesting as a species. How can this be wrong?

Any manager who fails to appreciate this is going to make very poor choices. There is no logical reason to assume that the most talented or productive people are those who are totally committed to their career. Their teams will exclude potentially stellar contributions from extremely talented and productive people who are willing to work hard all day because what they really want to do is something else all night and on weekends. Their teams will exclude the diverse perspectives brought by such people. They will waste a lot of money on incentive programs by falsely believing that the only way to motivate people is through monetary incentives.

Who makes the world go round? Certainly, the moneymakers and the people with power believe that they do. It is in their language. It is in how they speak. Our culture seems to elevate this view. However, anyone who reflects on the matter would realize that it is not only the moneymakers that make the world go round.

Sacagawea had neither money nor formal power in the expedition, yet in so many ways she was the one that "made the world go round." She did it for her own reasons and her acts of goodwill could not have been bought. So, at least of equal importance to the moneymakers and people with power are all the people who do many small and big things for no monetary gain. The people who do what they do out of love for what they do or out of love for others. Sure, it is the titans of industry that make the world go round. Sure, it is the senior executives of an organization. But we must understand that it is at least equally the teenage guitar teacher who spends a large part of her tuition fees baking cakes with her students after class. It is at least equally the old man in a wheelchair who smiles and waves to you from his porch whenever he sees you. It is at least equally the mother who makes a sacrifice for her child. As the gods of Olympus would have noticed, it is every single person who loves what they do, including the moneymakers, that makes the world go round.

12

Caesar Burns
All Doubt

| The Power of Making People Feel Safe |

Some two thousand years ago, the Roman Republic was mired in corruption. The Roman Senate had become jealous of one of their generals, Julius Caesar, a very popular military and political leader who expanded the borders of the Roman Republic through what are today France, Spain, and the island of Britain. On January 10th of 49 BC, Caesar, with his elite legion of soldiers, crossed the bridge over the Rubicon River to attack Rome and attempt to stamp out the corruption. What Caesar did next came as a surprise ...

A urelius stopped marching as he heard the drone of trumpets in the distance behind him. He knew this was a signal from the rear of his legion of troops that everyone had finished crossing the bridge over the river. His eyes traced the almost straight road that lay in front of him leading to the imperial city of Rome. The sun hung low on the horizon, casting long shadows over the outskirts of this ancient city. The air was heavy with anticipation as Julius Caesar and his seasoned army stood at the banks of the Rubicon River. It was eerily silent as a deep sense of foreboding filled the mind of each soldier with images of the bloody battle that lay ahead. The die had been cast, and a pivotal moment in history was about to unfold. Caesar's intent was clear: to march into Rome and confront the corrupt Senate, demanding reforms to root out the corruption that had plagued the heart of the Republic.

Aurelius, commander of the most elite legion in the Roman Republic, was a man known for his unwavering loyalty, courage, and strategic brilliance. As Caesar's gaze settled on the narrow bridge spanning the Rubicon, he gave the order that would define their destiny: "Burn the bridge behind us, Aurelius. There is no turning back."

Burn the bridge! echoed in Aurelius's mind. Slowly he turned to stare at the bridge, a flame of doubt dancing in his eyes. The weight of the order bore down on him, and he found himself at a moral cross-roads. To burn the bridge would be to expose his troops to a perilous fight from which they could not retreat—a journey that could end in death or charges of treason. He considered the lives and futures of the men he led, his responsibilities to them gnawing at his conscience.

I do not know if Caesar is right to burn the bridge, wondered Aurelius. He understood that Caesar gave the order to impress on his men the need for victory. Turning back would not be an option. To survive they had to win. He understood the logic, but he did not know that it was the best thing to do. His mind was confused, he did not know what was the best thing to do.

Thoughts of rebellion drifted into his mind. *Would the soldiers refuse to allow the bridge to be burned? Would they mutiny against Caesar? Dear God!* Aurelius thought. *Will I lead this mutiny?*

Yet, amid the turmoil of his thoughts, there was something that anchored Aurelius. He recalled the countless battles that he and many of the troops had fought together under Caesar, the hardships endured side by side, and the countless instances where Caesar had proven himself a fair and just leader. Trust had been forged in the crucible of adversity, and Aurelius knew that he could rely on Caesar, even when the path ahead seemed uncertain and perhaps bound for death.

It was this trust that resonated with Aurelius more than any strategic advantage or calculation. He knew that Caesar was not merely a conqueror, but a leader who deeply cared for his troops. The welfare of his men was as much a priority as the victory itself. This realization settled the moral dilemma that had clouded his mind. Trust was the anchor that steadied him, the compass that guided his decision. At that moment Aurelius resolved that the bridge would be burned.

He gathered his officers and soldiers and spoke with conviction. "Brothers, we stand at a crossroads, but fear not. Our leader, Julius Caesar, has led us through storms and victories alike. He has shown us fairness and valor, and he will ensure our safety even at the cost of his own life. Let us burn this bridge, not out of desperation but out of trust in the man who stands before us."

With unwavering resolve, Aurelius and his men set the bridge ablaze. The flames rose high, casting an eerie glow on the determined faces of the soldiers. It was more than a physical act; it was a symbol of their commitment, their steadfast faith in their leader.

As they marched toward Rome, the potential for death and sacrifice looming before them, their steps were not driven solely by the impossibility of retreat. It was the trust in Caesar that emboldened them, that transformed their fear into a resolute determination. The bridge had burned, but what truly mattered was the fire of trust that blazed within them.

 In the annals of history, the crossing of the Rubicon became a symbol of bold leadership and unshakable loyalty. Aurelius and his men faced the unknown with their heads held high, knowing that they were not

alone in their trials and tribulations. Their trust in Caesar had fortified them, reminding the world that trust—above all else—is the cornerstone of leadership that can change the course of history.

I am a great believer in the human spirit. I believe that people are inherently motivated, and once a leader can tap into this inherent spirit of motivation, great things can be accomplished. Many people begin their day by reading motivational stories or looking at motivational videos. Accumulating these sources of external motivation is obviously very beneficial. However, it is often overlooked that these motivational stories are at their most powerful when they unlock the readers' own internal motivation.

Leaders are critical to the degree of motivation of their followers, as they have the power to ignite the flame of greatness or snuff it out. I do not say this out of idealism or wishful thinking. It is an empirical fact. I certainly have, and I am sure we all have, seen occasions where people have blossomed once they have changed their environment and by dint of that change their leader. I am sure we would have all seen the performance of groups of people uplifted or crushed once their leader changes. We only have to study history, business, or current affairs to see examples of leaders, for better or for worse, transforming nations, battles, corporations, and sports teams.

The question then is, how can one man or woman have such an impact on so many people? The answer is that they don't, really. That is, they do not have a direct impact on most of the people that they lead. In the previous story, Caesar would have had a direct relationship with only a small percentage of his troops, yet he was a powerful leader. If successful leaders are not victims of narcissism, they will admit that there is nothing particularly special about them other than they understand that it is essential to create an environment or atmosphere for everyone to access their inner motivation. They understand that once such an atmosphere is created, it will propel each team member to strive, leading to the success of the entire team and the success of the leader. This is exactly what Caesar did when he burnt the bridge.

To create the correct environment, there are many things that these leaders intuitively or explicitly understand. The most important of these is that they understand that everyone has an innate and primal need to feel safe in the face of challenges or even danger. We are all very much aware of our basic material needs of food, water, and shelter. What we often overlook is that we also have a few basic emotional needs. I will not go over the list here, but perhaps the most primal of these is the need to feel safe.

This is not just a characteristic of human beings. It is a characteristic of life. This is at the core of the reason why fish swim in shoals, birds fly in flocks, and wildebeest move in herds. It is at the heart of why primitive man formed tribes then villages then towns then civilizations. Life inherently understands that there is safety in a collective. For order to emerge in a collective a leader is necessary. Originally leaders emerged by the will of the collective. In other words by some fashion of consensus. One of the key traits of such organic leaders is that, at some level, they make their followers feel safe. This trait is necessary for a leader to emerge and for that leader to hold on to power.

Once people feel safe, not just physically but emotionally, they switch into a superior mode of operation. Freed from the shackles of fear and anxiety, the tremendous power of their mind is unleashed. People can only be creative and inventive if they operate from a safe space. Once people realize that their own safety is dependent upon the existence of their collective, their team, they go out of the way to support and enhance their team whether this team is a club, corporation, or nation. Under the shelter of this collective, people take risks once they understand the rules under which their failures will be protected. Risks form the fertile soil on which grows the fruitive tree of reward and success.

In the commercial world, unless someone is a sole artisan, craftsman, or trader, he or she is forced to work within a team. For superior performance, it is critical that the leader of a business team cultivates an environment where team members feel safe. The most important requirement for achieving this is for the leader to be trusted by his team members. In short, for leaders to unlock the magnificent potential of their teams, they must earn the trust of each team member. Trust is like a forest; it will tend to naturally grow unless you do something to destroy it. I have seen many leaders fail because they have destroyed the trust and the goodwill of their team sometimes to the point where it creates the outright mutiny that the leader so richly deserves.

A sense of safety and a sense of trust are deeply interrelated. Anything a leader does that undermines the sense of safety destroys trust in the leader. As mentioned earlier, at a deep psychological level, people follow a leader because there is an unspoken covenant that the leader will keep them safe. It is this sense of safety that creates trust in a leader. As a consequence, a wise leader has a duty to be a ferocious protector of his or her team from the outside world. Once he or she does so it builds trust and loyalty. The most powerful way for a leader to destroy trust is to not accept blame personally and either implicitly or explicitly pass on blame to the team in general or to specific members of the team. This passing on of blame is the exact opposite of keeping people safe by protecting them from the outside world.

A proper leader is meant to be in control of how his or her team is constituted, equipped, and behaves. Therefore, when a leader does not accept personal responsibility for shortcomings of the team, apart from destroying the trust of team members, the leader is signaling ineptness and lack of control. The leader not only destroys the trust of his or her team but also the trust of his or her superiors. Quite a lose-lose situation is created. When a leader throws a team member under the proverbial bus, they should be aware that they do so by standing directly in the path of that bus.

This is not to say that a leader should tolerate blameworthy actions by members of the team. For a team to be a high-performing one, the leader must deal with any blameworthy behavior by specific team members, but they must do so within the confines of the team and not under the spotlight of the outside world. To preserve trust the leader must personally accept blame first, and then deal with the issues internally within the team. Once emotions die down, as they inevitably do, people understand and respect tough decisions made by a leader, as long as those decisions are fair, consistent, and transparent. Even people who are directly adversely affected by the tough decisions of a leader tend to respect that leader, as long as these conditions are met. However, if these conditions are not met—in other words, if a leader is unfair, dishonest, or not transparent—then trust is destroyed.

It is also true that trust is destroyed by a leader who garners too much credit and praise personally and limits attention to the contribution of the team as a whole. Team members feel that the spoils of victory are being stolen from them by their very own leader. They obviously react badly to this. Nor is it necessary for a leader to behave in such a manner, as it is understood that if team members are successful, then so is the team and so is the leader.

Great civilizations have been built upon the creation of a sense of safety that unlocks the human potential of their citizens. Leaders in the business world have a tremendous opportunity to similarly unlock the immense potential of their people if they understand the significance of safety and trust.

13

The Christmas Truce

The Wisdom of Loving People and Not Ideas

At the time, World War One was the most devastating war fought by humanity. Its scale was unprecedented, and it saw the introduction of the widespread use of mechanical warfare and a significant use of chemical weapons. The extent of the carnage was horrific. In large sectors of the battle theater, a stalemate arose leading to troops being forced to live in appalling conditions in trenches. Yet in the face of this horror, a miracle of sorts occurred on Christmas Eve 1914. The following is the true story ...

G raham Williams wasn't supposed to be here. The young rifleman in the 5th London Rifle Brigade had been anticipating a warm Christmas dinner in the relatively safe Belgian town of Ploegsteert this very night. Instead, a last-minute order sent him back into the muddy trenches, ducking sniper fire with his fellow disgruntled company mates. It was Christmas Eve, and Williams had just seen the skull of the boy beside him explode, victim to one of those apparitions with a scope perched two hundred yards across the corpse-filled expanse known as "no-man's land."

Meanwhile, John Ferguson was settling in for one more long night, having already served the entirety of his bid thus far along the Western Front. He rubbed warmth into his hands and anxiously awaited whatever fate this hell on Earth held for him, feeling the cold metal of his rifle between his hands and the lopsided helmet atop his head.

It was the last month of 1914. The Great War was in its infancy. At the time, what was thought would be a weeks-long skirmish was spiraling into a much longer endurance of carnage. It was certainly more misery than any of the men in these blood-soaked trenches had bargained for when they were sent into this mess.

The air smelled of death, the soggy soil increasingly pocked with explosions and bullets. The frontlines between the British and German forces in eastern France were a grim reminder of the horrors of war. But on this extraordinary Christmas Eve, a glimmer of humanity shone through the violence, proving that even the direst of human conflicts need not turn people into bitter, total enemies.

Williams could not help but wonder about the men on the other side of the barbed wire. Did they also long for home, for warmth, for peace?

Across the bleak field, Arno Böhme, a German infantryman, shared the same thoughts. He had left behind a family and a life he cherished to serve his country. But as the days turned into months, he began to question the killings, the seemingly bottomless dredge of suffering.

As Christmas Eve night approached, a peculiar quiet descended upon the battlefield. The guns and grenades fell silent, no racing footsteps of a nearby raid could be heard either. Instead, Williams and his fellow British soldiers heard the distant melody of "Silent Night" wafting through the air. They soon realized it was coming from the opposing trench line, where their German counterparts hunkered in their own filthy pits. Although the language was alien to the British men, it brought back memories of love and family for all of them, and they began to sing along in their own language. The magic of the song had a similar effect on scores of soldiers on both sides of the battle.

Curiosity and the desire for a brief respite from the horrors of war overcame the soldiers' initial apprehension. To his surprise and delight, Williams saw a line of candle lights appear just above the enemy's parapet. They were makeshift Christmas trees, a tradition held most strongly by the German troops.

Before anyone knew the impetus, more lights began to appear in the darkness, casting a soft glow on the frost-covered ground. Out of their common traditions of Christmas, a miraculous makeshift truce arose. "Out of the darkness," Ferguson later recalled, "we could hear laughter and see lighted matches, a German lighting a Scotsman's cigarette and vice versa, exchanging cigarettes and souvenirs."[1]

The sight of a German soldier was startling to Williams, and the appearance of a British soldier was equally surprising to Böhme. But as they cautiously exchanged greetings, they found common ground in their shared humanity.

They exchanged stories about their families, their hopes for the future, and their fears of it as well. They shared photographs and mementos from home, realizing that they were not so different after all.

Soldiers from both sides streamed out of their respective trenches for this impromptu gathering. They built makeshift Christmas trees from branches and adorned them with whatever they could find.

---

1   Jerome Gavin, "The Christmas truce," VisionofHumanity.org, accessed November 2023, https://www.visionofhumanity.org/the-christmas-truce/; "The Christmas truce of WWI as told by the soldiers who were there," TheWeek.com, accessed November 2023, https://theweek.com/world-news/first-world-war/61816/wwi-christmas-truce-soldiers-memories-of-the-brief-peace.

Cigarettes, buttons, chocolates, and even bottles of schnapps, gin, and whiskey were exchanged as gestures of goodwill.

The truce that no one expected quickly spread across the frontline. Soldiers who had been trying to kill each other mere hours earlier now played football, enjoyed a meal together, and sang carols in their native languages.

For a moment, the battlefield transformed into a place of camaraderie and unity. The soldiers on both sides buried their dead and tended to their wounded, using the surprising ceasefire to shore up their trenches as well. It was a testament to our innate desire to find common ground with our fellow person, to show mercy and charity even in times of unthinkable hardship and hatred.

As Christmas Day dawned, the truce came to an end, and the soldiers returned to their respective trenches. They knew that duty would once again call them to fight, but they also carried with them a newfound understanding of the kindness that existed on both sides of the war.

Graham and Arno, now forever connected by that extraordinary Christmas Eve, returned to their jobs as soldiers. They continued to fight, but with a deeper appreciation for the lives and similarities of the men they faced across no-man's land.

 The Christmas Truce of 1914 remains a poignant reminder of the potential for reconciliation and peace, even in the face of the gravest moments of conflict. It is a story of hope and resolution. It's a testament to the power empathy and compassion hold within us all, however untapped it may be.

I have always found the true story of the Christmas Eve Truce to be especially heart-rending. The most important lesson for me is that people do not want to be enemies with others, because deep within all of us we can always find something in common with other people. When "enmity" first rears its ugly head, it is usually in an emotionally charged atmosphere. Enmity causes people to do things that create misery. Perhaps this misery is nature's way of restoring balance because misery often causes reflection and leads us to realize that having enemies is hard and painful work!

Of course, enmity has degrees. At one extreme is warfare, like in the preceding story. At a lower degree, it is the distrust or dislike of people we see as opponents. Quite often this dislike arises for a simple and innocent reason, just because they do not agree with a point of view that we cherish.

Something that I heard a few decades ago has stuck in my memory because I found it to be a particularly strange statement at the time. I was in the process of buying my very first car, and I had just informed a car salesman that I had chosen to purchase another brand of car from another dealership. The salesman, who was much older than me, gently touched the side of my shoulder and said, "That's OK; it does not make you my enemy."

The salesman was polite, and we always had courteous interactions, so I wondered why the issue of enmity would even arise. Years later I realized that he understood human nature much better than I did at the time. Perhaps his choice of the word "enemy" was exaggerated, but he understood that people have an innate tendency to consider those who disagree with their taste or opinions as opponents or adversaries. In many circumstances, usually under stress or haste, people even treat an opponent or adversary as an enemy. It is funny that the root of this "enmity" is, in fact, love. Love of an idea. We tend to fall in love with ideas, and it is indeed true that love and hate are opposite poles of the same thing.

We are very conscious of our physical world, and we are usually aware when we fall in love with a person, an animal, or an object. However, most of the time we are unaware that in our mental world we also fall in love with ideas. We fall in love with our mental maps that we discussed a few chapters before. Ideas are part of the conduit between that which we imagine and that which we make real. They are very powerful things, and when mixed with ethics and morality, they are very good things. However, like all that is powerful, they come with associated dangers. In the case of ideas, the key danger is in loving them too much.

Love is blind. When we love something, we tend not to see its imperfections. We defend it furiously even when we should not. The problem with ideas is that they are formed out of human intelligence, which is not perfect. As human beings we possess neither absolute knowledge, infinite mental capacity, nor limitless experience. An idea is therefore always incomplete and imperfect. It is always a piece of an even bigger construct. There is always a better one. Even when an idea is excellent, it is only so within a particular context, place, or time. They grow old quickly and lose potency when they move from circumstance to circumstance. So being in love with an idea is being in love with something that is fundamentally incomplete and imperfect. Unless we are conscious of this, it can invoke many of our base emotions and lead us to think warlike thoughts against those who do not similarly love our idea.

Apart from disturbing our human interactions, loving an idea too much can limit our own creativity. It can blind us to better ideas, causing us to miss superior options and more profitable opportunities. In many cases when we believe we are open-minded to new ideas, what we really mean is that we are open-minded to ideas that resemble the ones that we already love. With this approach you will miss all the benefits of looking at a situation from a diametrically different angle. If you look at the consequences objectively, it is dangerous at many levels.

At the most personal level, it limits you. This is because it cuts you off from a universe of opportunities, some of which may enrich your life financially or emotionally. The people who make inordinate profits on the stock market are generally those who do not share the same ideas as the masses. They run differently from the herd. It can also limit your growth in your career. In almost every office there is an office dinosaur who is bypassed by his colleagues and bypassed for promotions because his approach to things stopped being current a long time ago. No one wants to interact with him as they see him as too closed-minded.

Being in love with the ideas in our heads leads to the propensity for many leaders to select team members of very similar thought patterns. They form a club of people with a shared love. This might be sensible for a stamp-collecting club, but for a commercial enterprise, this is totally counterproductive, as the collective mind of the team becomes not much more expansive than the mind of each team member. Just as entire crops of the same genetic type are prone to eradication by a single disease, such teams run the risk of being blindsided by situations and events that they had not envisaged. The tendency to think of diversity in terms of gender, race, ethnicity, and orientation is valuable but perhaps of at least equal value is diversity of thought.

It is very easy to fall into the weakness of hating things that are significantly dissimilar to those that we love. This is the basis of outright animosity to people who do not share our opinions. It is a form of bigotry that is easy to mask as it is not evident on the surface. However, apart from being patently unfair, this thought pattern undermines our own success. To a very large part, success is based upon human interaction and the ability to understand other human beings. A stubborn refusal to examine and consider opposing points of view is an artificial barrier to this natural process of human understanding and human interaction. It narrows our perspective and significantly weakens our ability to influence people and to lead teams. It diminishes our charisma. This is exactly the point that the salesman was making to me a long time ago. Someone who disagreed with him was not his enemy. It took me more than twenty years to understand the wisdom of his words.

Ideas are not people. You cannot hurt their feelings. They do not have an intrinsic life. We give life to them. We do not need to be loyal to ideas, but we so often are. People fall into the trap of hanging on to old ideas that are no longer relevant because they feel that they have invested too much time in developing and expanding on these ideas. There is especially the danger of this happening in academia where the investment of time can span generations of careers. It is brave to discard entrenched ideas in such circumstances, as often people who do so are attacked by their own colleagues. However, the rewards can be amazing. This is exactly how truly revolutionary inventions and discoveries occur.

A hermit crab does not hesitate to discard its shell and find a new one if it has outgrown the old shell. I have never understood why many people, on the contrary, seem ashamed to admit that they have given up an old idea and adopted a better one. Perhaps they believe that it is an admission that they were wrong. However, this is totally not the case. It does not imply that they were wrong in the past. What it signifies is that they are smart enough to know that if they continue with the old way of thinking they would be wrong in the future. Perhaps they believe that it makes them look indecisive. Nothing can be further from the truth as it is an act of boldness and true leadership. It is supreme decisiveness.

The soldiers on that Christmas Eve night in 1924 showed love and compassion to each other. Humans are worthy of love, ideas are not. This fundamental truth shone so brightly on that night so long ago when the love for what all the soldiers had in common made them forget whatever ideas they were even fighting over. Most of the time loving an idea is a symptom of narcissism, since ideas become part of us; so loving them is, in fact, loving ourselves more than others. Use ideas, but discard them in a heartbeat when you discover a better one. They are not real. They have no feelings. Too many people wrongly do this with people and too few people rightly do this with ideas. There is great power in mastering the art of swapping ideas when an old one no longer fits.

14

Orestes Breaks
a Curse

The Powerful Spell of
Self-Responsibility and Saving

*In Greek mythology, Orestes was Prince of Argos, son of Agamemnon —
the city's beloved king and hero of the Trojan War. His mother
Clytemnestra, though, was of an entirely different character. Life
changed for Orestes through no fault of his own, and he was placed
in a seemingly impossible moral dilemma. Would he be a victim
of circumstances or take responsibility for his situation?*

O restes stood on the rocky cliffs overlooking the tumultuous
sea, the salty air stinging his face. The sun dipped low on
the horizon, casting long shadows on the ancient land of his
ancestral home, Argos. Orestes had always known the weight of his
name. He'd heard the whispers in the seamy corners of the city, the
hushed tales of blood and betrayal that clung to the House of Atreus,
his familial clan, like a curse. The ghosts of his family's sins hovered
over him like a shroud. His mother's conniving blade had silenced
his father, the great warrior and Trojan conqueror Agamemnon. It

was the duty demanded of a son to slay his father's killer, but Orestes could not bring himself to kill his mother. Matricide was the gravest of sins in the eyes of the gods, and the impossible dilemma had forced Orestes to abandon the city and his birthright.

Over the years of his self-imposed exile, he wandered in poverty through distant lands, seeking a path to redemption for the inherited sins that so mercilessly invaded his thoughts—that of his mother, and his own guilt for neither protecting nor avenging his father. Seven years later he decided that the time had come to somehow find a way to make things right, not only for his father but for the people of Argos as well. He returned to Argos, a drifter in his own city, lost amid those whispers and rumors. The town, once vibrant with life and commerce, had withered under the greed-driven rule of his mother Clytemnestra and her lover, Aegisthus.

Orestes entered a dimly lit tavern in Argos, its patrons casting wary glances at the returning son of a murdered king and an unpopular queen. They saw him, and then they ignored him. Orestes was the son of the mighty Agamemnon, but he knew they defined him as a coward, someone who shared the moral complexion of his mother. He ordered a simple meal of lamb and bread with a glass of ouzo, their earthy flavors bringing him a small measure of solace.

As he ate, a grizzled fisherman named Nikos sat down beside him. "You're the young man who's come back to reclaim his name," Nikos muttered. There was a hint of sympathy in his weathered eyes.

Orestes nodded, his jaw clenched. "Yes, my own name ... my family name ... I'm not sure anymore."

Nikos leaned closer, his voice a low rumble. "I've seen the waves swallow many a man, son. Revenge is a tempestuous sea, and it can drown a soul just as easily as a ship."

"You seem to know my intentions in coming here, old man. How so?"

Nikos laughed. "I've spent many more years on this world than you, my boy. And I've seen many more things, too. It's not the first look of vengeance I've watched ponder across a young man's face."

Orestes thought for a moment. "All of Argos think I am a coward. Perhaps vengeance will redeem me. Is that bad? Tell me then, old man, in all your wisdom. What should I do?"

"The biggest coward is someone who does not take responsibility, blames the past, blames other people. You must take responsibility for your past—yours and your family's," Nikos answered. "Make peace with it before the regret swallows you whole."

Orestes swirled his cup and stared into his ouzo. "You want me to take responsibility, but my mother plotted with her lover and put my father in his grave, yet I just watch on at their despicable rule over my father's city. How do I find redemption?"

Nikos raised a calloused hand, fingers gnarled like driftwood. "Ah, redemption. A rare feat, rarest of them all perhaps. With care, my boy. That's what you need. Thoughtfulness of all opportunities beyond crass vengeance and the choices that come along with them. Just as a fisherman repairs his nets today to ensure a fruitful catch tomorrow, you must mend your past deeds to catch what you need for your future."

The words hung heavy in the air, and Orestes felt a flicker of realization. His quest wasn't about vengeance or forgiveness; it was about not blaming his present and his future on his past. It was about moving on.

He had always been a man of few words, a trait he had inherited from his father. "Actions speak louder than words." His father had drilled the phrase into his memory. He could not undo the past, but he could shape the future by taking the next right step now, followed by another.

As he sipped his ouzo, Orestes thought about his mother, Clytemnestra. She has always been clever and resourceful, always finding a way to get what she wanted. But she had used those qualities to satisfy her lust for power. Orestes vowed to use them differently.

Fortune favors those who take action. On leaving the tavern and wandering the dark streets of Argos pondering his options, Orestes had a chance encounter with an old ally, his cousin Pylades. Pylades still held influence with the generals of Argos and, like Orestes, was sickened by the rule of Clytemnestra. They shared a common goal. If Pylades was to succeed in ousting Clytemnestra, he needed to support someone like Orestes with a claim on the throne, and Orestes needed Pylades for his military influence. Together, they devised a plan to confront the demons of the past, and with them the guilt that had weighed so heavily on Orestes all these years.

Orestes knew that he had to take responsibility for his lack of action in the past. He couldn't deny the darkness within him any longer. He and Pylades marshaled the support of the mighty army of Argos and stormed into the palace, confronting Clytemnestra and Aegisthus. With his eyes locked onto his mother's, Orestes spoke with such power, his words strong and true, that his voice cut through the air like a blade.

"I am Orestes, son of Agamemnon. I have come to end this treachery."

The room hung in silence, the tension palpable. Clytemnestra, cunning as she was, saw the shadow of her past cast upon her. She knew that justice demanded reckoning. She was terrified, as she knew that Orestes had finally come to avenge his father, her crimes inescapable now.

Orestes, his sword weighing on his hand, wrestled with the guilt that threatened to consume him, but he chose a different path. Instead of vengeance, he opted for fairness. He did not slay Clytemnestra and Aegisthus where they stood, but allowed the people of Argos to act as jurors, casting aside the cycle of gory revenge that had plagued his family for generations.

Clytemnestra and Aegisthus were found guilty, their fate sealed by the very people they had ruled through greed and deceit. Orestes exiled her from Argos. Clytemnestra, once the crafty queen, left as a shell, forced to find her own path to redemption.

But Orestes did not find solace in his victory. He realized that his struggle had not only been in facing the consequences of his actions but also in breaking free from the curse that had bound his family. He realized that he needed to choose a different path for himself, one of reconciliation and healing where he defined himself by his own deeds and not by the sins of his ancestors. He knew he had to fight to create his own future, one of measured decisions, a life less burdened by the mistakes of his past.

Orestes's return and inheritance of the throne had transformed Argos. The people saw in him a symbol of hope, and over time they judged him as his own man, no longer as a scion of the wicked Clytemnestra. He worked tirelessly to restore peace and harmony to Argos, seeking forgiveness from the gods for the blood that had been shed in his name.

 Today, the story of Orestes serves as a timeless reminder of the important strength of personal responsibility. It teaches us that true redemption lies not in seeking vengeance or in following the codes written by circumstances but in taking responsibility for our actions and working toward a better future for ourselves and those within our charge. Orestes broke the succession of violence and, in doing so, proved that the power to change one's destiny lies within the choices we make in the here and now and the responsibility we ultimately accept for them.

Ancestral sins had made life unfair for Orestes. He had no control over the deeds of his mother, yet he suffered for her sins. In the real world, it is easy to think of many things that are similarly unfair due to difficult circumstances created beyond someone's control. Sometimes the person involved can laugh it off, but often the situation is tragic. The extent of bad luck can be amazing. I have read of a former park ranger from Virginia who was struck by lightning seven times over his lifetime. A woman from Alabama was hit by a meteorite in 1954. Such random acts of happenstance occur every day that can change the trajectory of one's life. And on the economic front, we can see examples of unfairness and bad luck anywhere we look. Some are born into wealth while others are born into poverty. Some are born in an environment where opportunities are easily accessible while others are born in an environment where it is a struggle, even for the smallest of opportunities. William Blake captured it in his poem, "Auguries of Innocence," as:

"Every Night and every Morn
Some to Misery are born.
Every Morn and every Night
Some are born to Sweet Delight...
Some are born to Endless Night."

I raise these sad matters to make the point that neither nature nor life has to be inherently fair. For some people it is, for others it is not. This is a simple fact. Sometimes circumstances change over time. Orestes was born into luxury as a prince, yet he had to wander in exile through no real fault of his own. The issue is not whether economic unfairness exists, as no one can argue that it does not. The issue rather is whether there is an approach to overcome it. That answer is a resounding "yes."

Across the world there are myths and stories about people who could cast spells and people who were the victims of spells. There is no evidence left in the modern world to suggest that spells have ever existed in reality. However, I would argue that there are certain attitudes that could be imprinted on people that would have the same impact on them as if they were the victims of a spell. Conferring a mental attitude on someone is no different in substance to casting a spell on them. If I wanted to achieve the equivalent of casting the "spell of poverty" on someone, I would convince them that their problems are someone else's fault and that putting aside savings has no value.

Self-responsibility is a very powerful mindset. But what does self-responsibility actually mean? It means that we deal with a situation personally regardless of whether or not we believe it is our fault or that the situation has arisen from rotten luck. If we have self-responsibility, we do not waste our time ruing our misfortunes. We understand that fault is irrelevant and that what is relevant is that we take personal action.

By way of a trivial example just to make the point, suppose that you had a report due in an hour, and while you went to get a cup of coffee, a horrible fellow employee threw a candy wrapper on your keyboard. You have two choices. You can leave the wrapper there, letting it bother you as you try to type around the wrapper, or you can toss the wrapper into the bin and get on with your report. I do not need to point out which is the more productive option. Faces do not look good without noses, yet so many people cut off their noses to spite their faces.

Although this example is a trivial one, it illustrates the point that when someone is in a bad situation that is the deliberate or accidental fault of others, the best approach is to take ownership of the situation and personally take action to overcome it. Often this is the only approach with any chance of success, as waiting for the person at fault to take action puts the victim at the mercy of the perpetrator.

To supercharge self-responsibility, one should go a step further than taking action to overcome a situation that is the fault of others. One should act as if it is their own fault! That is correct, act as if it is your own fault! This is very powerful, because it completes a mental circuit where you take ownership for both cause and effect, just as Orestes took personal responsibility for restoring Argos to its former glory. It puts mental pressure to discover solutions to the issue and it creates tremendous energy to take action. Note that I am not saying that you should accept blame for the actions of the perpetrator. All I am saying is to take action *as if* it were your fault. Orestes became a hero of Argos when he stopped taking blame for the deeds of Clytemnestra and instead took responsibility for fixing all that she had done as if it were his own fault.

The second component of the spell of poverty is the mentality of not understanding the value of putting aside savings, which can only be achieved by spending less than you earn, in other words by being thrifty. I recall that when on a trip to Egypt over a decade ago, I was warned about the abject poverty I would see in certain parts of Cairo. When I visited these parts of Cairo, I did see people with few material possessions, but they seemed no less happy than anyone else. They were certainly kind and friendly. What I took away from the visit was not their poverty but their warmth. My point is that there is not necessarily a correlation between wealth and happiness. Sure, I know many wealthy people who are very happy, but I also know many wealthy people who are very sad. I know many less-wealthy people who are miserable, but I also know many less-wealthy people who are happy. The lesson about being thrifty is to understand that as you earn more, spending the extra that you earn does not necessarily make you that extra bit happier. What it most often does is put you into an economic trap where you believe that you can never earn enough.

When people earn little, they are forced spend it all on food, housing, and other necessities. As they start to earn a bit more, their standard of living increases. And as they continue to earn more and more, there comes a point where they have a choice to make. They could continue to expand their lifestyle to fit their income, or they could allow their income to grow faster than their lifestyle. The former is a trap—the trap of falling into a never-ending cycle of thinking that they do not earn enough to rise above their circumstances. This is the very opposite of being thrifty. A key ingredient of achieving economic progress is having the discipline to allow your income to exceed your lifestyle. The buffer between income and lifestyle provides an arsenal to create financial security in case life becomes unfair or to overcome the financial unfairness to which you may have already been subjected.

Neither nature nor life is inherently fair, but they provide the tools to allow someone a chance to overcome this unfairness. Life is a journey, and if the start of the journey was not desirable, and the end is inevitably uncertain, then the onus is on us to enjoy the part of the journey in between as we practice self-responsibility and being thrifty to create the life that we desire.

15

How Much Gold Can Attila the Hun Carry?

| Why Purpose Is Key |

From 434 AD, Attila was king of the Huns, a nomadic people from Central Asia and the Caucasus. During his twenty-year reign, he relentlessly sacked and slaughtered town after town in his endless pursuit of plunder. He was one of the most feared enemies of both the Eastern and Western Roman Empires. To this day his name is synonymous with anyone who is a terrifying invader. Details of his death are unclear, but it is widely believed that he died while celebrating his latest marriage to Ildico, a Gothic maiden. In this story we'll speculate on how he specifically died, and what may have been his final thoughts ...

A s he noticed that he was becoming weaker and was losing consciousness, an image from so long ago, when he was but a child, drifted into his mind. It was of Beku, his father's servant, always wearing tattered rags. Attila had not thought of Beku for almost a lifetime, so he wondered why he thought of him now. In his memory he could see Beku's old, craggy face softly saying, "How much gold can an old man carry?" Even though he was no more than six years old at the time, Attila remembered thinking that Beku was a foolish old man with no gold, not even a grain of gold dust to carry, so of course he would say something like that.

Attila had built his life around carrying gold. Taking over from where their father had left off, Attila and his brother Bleda as joint kings of the Huns sacked, looted, and pillaged town after town. The death of Bleda gave Attila sole dominion over the Huns, and in his grief the ferocity of his attacks grew. He saw towns as trophies that he would make flow a river of blood to acquire. His ever-growing army followed a pattern. They would slaughter every last man, and after they looted everything of value, they would burn the buildings. They did not slaughter the children and young or pretty women, not out of kindness but out of avarice and lust. Beautiful women and healthy youths were of great value to be sold as slaves—more gold for him to carry.

Laying on his bed now, a sharp, intense pain ripped through Attila's stomach. A pain that would make an ordinary man scream, but he was king of the Huns, so he would not allow himself to scream. As he felt blood seep down his nostrils onto his silken sheets, memories of his mother flooded Attila's mind. Hilda was a beautiful woman. One with a kind heart and a gentle manner. Hilda was the diametric opposite of Attila's father, a cold, cruel brute. Although she suffered greatly in her marriage, Hilda carried herself with poise and dignity. When his father was not around, Hilda would take the child Attila to see farmers tend to their crops. The Huns were nomads, never staying anywhere long enough to plant crops, yet Attila remembered that his childhood fantasy was to be a farmer. He remembered how happy those times were spent with his mother. As his breathing became more difficult, he realized that though he chose to live his life in cruelty, because of those days he knew what it meant to be loved. Without success he tried to fight memories from filling his mind, memories of the blood of farmers and of farms in flames. Memories of screaming women being dragged into captivity. He realized that these memories were more painful than what he felt in his stomach.

With effort Attila opened his damp eyes. The first thing he saw was the golden treasure that was kept in his tent, just part of the fortune he had pillaged over his life. He heard rapid breathing and looked to his side. There she was, his new bride Ildico, staring at him with a look of satisfaction on her face.

Alaric, a Gothic chieftain, had resisted Attila's armies for years, but like so many before, they too were crushed. Alaric pleaded with Attila to spare his surviving people. He promised that in return he would pledge loyalty to Attila, and to prove his loyalty he gave his only daughter, Ildico, in marriage to Attila to be yet another of his brides.

Attila sensed that this may have been a trap, but he ignored his instincts. A younger Attila would have been on his guard around Ildico, but he no longer cared. Attila had long realized that his life was an endless cycle of slaughter and plunder. When he was young, he thought that the gold he garnered would make him happy, but he now knew that that was not true. Years ago he realized that he could see no purpose to what he did, but he was king of the Huns; this life was all he knew, so he continued with his relentless pursuit of wealth, though he grew weary of it.

Attila looked at Ildico's beautiful face. Behind her satisfaction he saw hatred in her eyes. In a mocking voice she said, "Are you enjoying your wedding night, my lord?"

She laughed loudly and began to tell Attila what he already knew. He knew it was likely to happen since he accepted Alaric's proposal, but he no longer concerned himself with death, as his life had long lost all purpose.

Ildico continued sharply, "You murdered my people, my family. You thought you were invincible, above justice, but I have made you pay. You cruel fool. You did not even realize I poisoned your wine."

Returning to her mocking voice, she said, "Close your eyes, Attila. This is the wedding night you deserve!"

She again laughed loudly. Attila felt sorrow for her. Sorrow for what his actions had made her do, sorrow for what he did to her and her people. Most of all he felt sorrow for his wasted life.

Ildico's shrill laughter attracted Attila's guards. They burst into the tent to see Attila lying helpless with blood oozing from his nose and mouth. Their instincts were that Ildico must be to blame. Realizing this, Attila weakly said, "My time is gone, brothers. An old battle wound has ruptured inside my stomach."

Looking at a surprised Ildico, he muttered almost inaudibly, "My bride has tried her best to tend to my wounds."

As his eyes closed for the final time, the last thing that they saw was his treasure of gold. Again he remembered Beku's words, "How much gold can an old man carry?" With his dying breath, he knew the answer: none. The answer for each of us is none, for in our final breath when we are at our oldest, we can carry nothing but our soul.

 As you may have noticed a number of times in this book, sometimes a major life lesson can be gleaned from something that is trivial on the surface, for example, trips to and from the airport. I love driving to the airport to go on a vacation. There is a sense of excitement and anticipation of all the fun things to do on the trip. But even if the vacation was wonderful, as it usually is, the drive back from the airport is never quite as enjoyable. Sure, there may be a sense of satisfaction and relaxation, which is delightful, but something seems missing compared

to the drive to the airport. That missing ingredient is a sense of purpose. There was a purpose to the outward trip. The return is just that, a return to the normal. It's a trip with an absence of purpose.

Having a sense of purpose fulfills us. It is not just that it makes us happy. Happiness is not the correct word. It is deeper than happiness. Having a purpose is a primal need that most of us feel; it is a hole that we try to fill. Anything that gives us purpose makes us feel good. In the story, Attila realized that his life was pointless when he realized that it had no purpose.

Nature is a magnificent teacher; we just have to observe. If we pay attention, we will notice that a sense of purpose is inherent to life. The sense of purpose for a wild animal is to eat, to not be eaten, and to reproduce. A tree gets a sense of purpose by managing its water, nutrients, and leaves to reach higher and higher toward the sun.

As humans, for the most part our basic biological needs are satisfied. Yet we crave a sense of purpose. We are complicated beings with a soul, whether you see that as something spiritual or something biochemical. We are so complicated that for most of us our sense of purpose is not fulfilled by eating, surviving, and reproducing, not at a higher level anyway.

One of the greatest problems facing humanity on an individual level is that we are so complicated that we cannot figure out what gives us a sense of purpose. It is like having an itch but not knowing where to scratch. The problem is that how we scratch this itch is personal to each of us. There is no right or wrong answer. We are all just wired differently.

Have you ever seen a cat walking along the top of a wall and slip and fall to the ground? It always manages to land on its feet, but it gets wide-eyed, confused, then it panics and scampers away to where it believes safety lies. In a sense we are like that cat. When we cannot find our purpose or it disappears, we are confused and scamper toward the closest thing that resembles a sense of purpose, because life is not fulfilling without one. The problem is that we struggle knowing in which direction to go, because life is mysterious, and it often does not easily reveal the secret of our true purpose.

For many of us, the default direction we take is the one where acquiring wealth becomes our objective. If we have no better answer, it is logical to assume that we will find a sense of purpose from acquiring wealth. After all, the needs to survive and to reproduce are primal. If we acquire wealth, it fulfills these needs. For some, this is enough to create a feeling of contentment, but not for all of us. For many there is still a craving.

Some try to find their purpose by doubling down on the accumulation of wealth. In fact, this is probably the natural thing to do. There is absolutely nothing wrong with this, as long as it is done in an honorable and ethical way. However, it is despicable if it is done in a selfish, cruel, and greedy manner as Attila the Hun did it. Some people do find their reason for being in making more money. I know many very wealthy people who enjoy life most when pursuing their commercial ventures. Though I notice that in these cases, it tends to be the act of running a successful commercial venture that gives them fulfillment more than the money made as the outcome. However, for many people this is still not enough. Like Attila, once "all that money can buy" is tasted, life loses its sweetness. And even though, unlike Attila, someone may make their money honorably, they can also start to wonder, "How much gold can an old man carry?" Sadly, these people often fall into the trap described in the previous chapter of allowing their lifestyle to always keep up with or exceed their income.

The million-dollar question therefore is, "How do I find my sense of purpose?" The answer is clearly, "It depends." The answer has to be "it depends," because individuality is intrinsic to being human. We have complicated minds with different likes, dislikes, wants, and needs. No two humans are the same. Therefore, what gives one person a sense of purpose would not necessarily give another person the same feeling.

While I cannot tell anyone what their main motivation in life is or should be, I can say that whatever it is, it must have one particular ingredient: service. The human animal craves a sense of purpose. However, also as deeply, the human animal craves to provide service and to help others! This is a fact. People feel good when they help others. Think about how good helping or providing service to someone makes you feel, even if you do so in a small way.

In fact, the craving for a sense of purpose is the flip side to the craving to provide service. Finding the activity that joins the two is a mystery that we each must individually solve. In doing so, we must not fall into the trap of assuming that the solution is just one activity. Perhaps it is in doing a few different activities that a sense of purpose is built, layer by layer.

There is a very powerful management lesson in the fact that someone's sense of purpose can be achieved by doing a number of different activities. People are extremely motivated, conscientious, and energetic if they are fulfilling their aspirations. The lesson is, therefore, that if we can run our business in a manner that adds to the sense of purpose of our employees, it will create superior performance.

An employer cannot reasonably expect that the life goal of their employees is to make the employer's business successful. That is patently empty-headed, even though a number of employers act this way. However, if an employer can give a sense of purpose to what their employees do, then it will foster a workforce of exceptional performance. This is achieved if a company has a powerful vision.

"Mission statements" and "vision statements" are commonly used interchangeably and usually a company only has one such thing that they call a mission statement or a vision statement. However, as management guru Adrian Schweizer pointed out to me many years ago, whatever you call them, there should be two of them that coexist. The two form a hierarchy. The higher of the two speaks to what the company does for others (which he calls the vision statement) and the lower of the two speaks to what the company does for itself (which he calls the mission statement). Providing a purposeful work experience that creates exceptional performance comes mainly from the vision statement and not as much from the mission statement.

For example, a valid mission statement may be something like, "To provide exceptional profits and be in the top five largest companies in our industry by revenue." This might excite the shareholders but would excite few employees. However, if that same company also had as a vision statement, "To bring the joy of beautiful music to as many people as possible by crafting exceptional guitars at an economical price," then the company has the ingredients for a motivated workforce.

Aristotle said that to know oneself is the beginning of all wisdom. This chapter delves deeply into knowing oneself. I believe that it is obvious to most that by definition fulfillment can only be achieved if we have a sense of purpose. If we have no purpose, what is there to fulfill? What is perhaps less obvious is that we all have an innate need to serve. This is powerful knowledge, as "the need to serve" is the key that nature has provided to unlock the discovery of our individual sense of purpose. The need to serve and to have a sense of purpose are interrelated, and satisfying one helps to satisfy the other.

At an individual level, there is magic in searching for the activities that bridge the two, and once we search for purpose with the sense of service in mind, we will usually discover purpose. Atilla could not succeed at having a purposeful life no matter how much gold he carried, because his life was completely bereft of service. Perhaps at last he briefly found a bit of purpose by serving his wife Ildico when he did not betray her to his soldiers.

Every one of us is on a quest: a quest for meaning, a quest for purpose. No worthy quest is easy, but armed with a sense of service, we are much more likely to succeed.

A Journey's End

You have joined me on a series of adventures through this book, and in a sense, through my life and career. As we traveled through the realms of career success, we explored a rich tapestry of wisdom drawn from history, mythology, and the lives of remarkable individuals. You have also heard personal stories of my life and from my time as a CEO working to grow a large company. I have drawn from my successes and, more importantly, from my failures. I hope that by sharing my experiences you will be inspired as you continue on your own career path.

As I have mentioned in the introduction, small changes to our attitudes and to how we approach our career and life often have massive impacts on our success. The purpose of each chapter is to bring out one such attitude or approach.

In each chapter, I have either challenged a notion that many people take for granted or suggested an approach that seems trivial but in fact has a massive impact on success. I want to leave you with a review of the main principles we covered, so you can more easily carry them with you and put them into action in your own life and work.

Our travels have been guided by the stories of incredible figures and legendary events, each illuminating a unique facet of the principles that underpin a prosperous career.

The story of Cristobal teaches us that being decisive is often superior to striving for unattainable perfection. Sometimes, the perfect decision is simply the one we make in the first place. Failure is inevitable; we all fail some of the time. This issue is not failure itself but what we gain because of failure. We are less likely to admit and accept our own failures if we perceive failure as a terrible thing that should be avoided at all costs. Such a mindset will paralyze you with fear, meaning you will fail to make any decision when you need to. By all means, do your best to mitigate risk, but understand that failure will always be a possibility with any decision you make.

Sir Walter Raleigh thought that he already knew everything, so he failed to detect the small snippets of information that would have unveiled his "El Dorado." The story reminds us that recognizing our gaps in knowledge is a strength, not a weakness. The power of humility lies in the recognition that there's always more to learn. Great leaders discern their strengths and aren't shy about admitting their weaknesses. They know that by admitting them they can leverage their weaknesses to better focus on their strengths.

Count St. Germain had infinite time, so he had no need to make life decisions. But Helene, like the rest of us, needed to make decisions and move on with her life. Her character urges us to transcend the limitations of the mind, to embrace a deeper understanding of our decisions, and to let intuition guide us when the path forward is unclear as it quite often is. We cannot predict every outcome, but we can move with the confidence that every decision can be overcome. The mind is far from perfect. It views the past inaccurately and usually with bias. It sees the future by projecting imaginary scenarios that may never come to pass. It is therefore very limiting to use our mind as our only decision-making organ. Trust the other parts of your intellect— your instincts, your will, your subconscious, and your "soul"—to make and follow through with your decisions. If the decisions you make today go awry later, believe in yourself that you will have time to right the ship before it sinks.

The clash of Hernando de Soto and Tuskaloosa at the Battle of Mabila reveals that humility is a cornerstone of success, that if someone is too proud to retreat, it can lead to devastating consequences. It is in understanding our vulnerability as leaders that we and our teams are made stronger. As a leader you become so much more powerful by admitting your limitations and acknowledging the contributions of others. A good leader must be relatable and approachable and very open to listening to advice.

Medusa was not simply a Gorgon. Had she used her great power for good she might have been seen more of a goddess. At one stage in her life, she was just a happy, innocent girl. Like Medusa we all have many facets, and who we become depends on the choices we make. We need to be vigilant not to make the choices that make us monsters. Medusa's surrender to Perseus highlights the importance of empathy. Her fate reminds us that unchecked power can transform us into monsters. Avoid becoming a monster by seeing the humanity in others, even in those who may seem adversarial.

The Bread Seller of Old Cairo showcases the sublime and universal power of generosity. The incredible return on investment that comes from giving more than expected is vital in any business, underscoring the significance of exceeding client and colleague expectations. It shows that "giving" does not have to cost much, yet the returns can be tremendous.

Leonardo da Vinci demonstrates the art of deploying diverse forms of intelligence as needed, understanding that versatility is a hallmark of brilliance. Da Vinci's mastery of various forms of intelligence encourages us to diversify our skill sets as different situations demand different forms of intelligence. We should cultivate and value not only academic intelligence but also observational and creative intelligence to name a few.

The story of the Gemini Twins illustrates the value of knowing that victory isn't always measured by tangible gains. Sometimes, it's wiser to accept a temporary loss to achieve a greater victory down the road. We should never fall into the addiction of chronically needing to win. True champions know when to win just as they know when to lose.

The cautionary tale of Procrustes warned us against the grave danger of assuming that our mental models of the world are correct. Many times, we believe that our accumulated knowledge already perfectly describes a situation, but more commonly than not this is not true. We need to see the world as it is, not as it must be if our ideas are to be true. We must not invent solutions before we understand the problem. Embrace diversity and adaptability, rather than trying to force everyone into one mold.

Arachne taught us the virtues of not becoming so enamored by our talent that we believe that we alone can do something well. It shows that as a leader you must have the humility to accept blame on behalf of the team, to delegate tasks, trust your team, and be accountable for the outcome.

The life of Sacagawea revealed that people have many other drivers than financial ones and that, in any particular situation, we should not assume that the person to bring the most value is the one with the most formal authority. Sacagawea's loyalty to her mission underscores the significance of purpose and respect in the workplace. Foster an environment where people feel valued, and their dedication will be a tremendous asset.

Julius Caesar's crossing of the Rubicon underscored the power of trust in leadership. People have an inherent desire to feel safe, and there is always an unwritten covenant that leaders will keep their followers safe. Creating an environment where people feel secure will lead to extraordinary accomplishments, as people will feel comfortable to innovate and will fight ferociously for the success of their team.

The Christmas Truce of World War One exemplified the wisdom of valuing people over ideologies, proving that humanity and compassion have the power to transcend even the darkest of times. We have a tendency to fall in love with our ideas to our detriment, since ideas are almost always incomplete and quickly become outdated. The story shows us the power of knowing when to discard ideas that we may have once loved.

Orestes reminded us of the need for self-responsibility, emphasizing that owning our choices is the first step toward redemption. Acknowledge your mistakes, learn from them, and use them to fuel your growth. Life is not always fair, and circumstances are often out of our control. What is in our control is what we do about them. Taking responsibility for our circumstances, along with not falling into the trap of allowing our lifestyle to keep pace with our income are the cornerstones of economic progress.

Attila the Hun showed us the emptiness of insatiable greed and the fulfillment found in a higher purpose. Attila's commitment to needless conquest only led him to a regretful end, a fate that serves as a stark reminder that fulfillment comes from more than wealth or power. We have both an innate need to provide service and to have a sense of purpose. They are interrelated as satisfying one helps to satisfy the other. Make your business purposeful and you will create a powerful workforce.

As we conclude our journey, my hope is that these tales and themes serve as your compass as you move toward your career and life goals. Practicing them would greatly enhance your chance of career success and, at the very least, would create a business landscape where people have greater empathy, compassion, and respect for each other.

The lessons in this book are not only applicable to the workplace but to life in general, as they would help to construct healthier interpersonal relationships and a more positive approach to life. Forge ahead with decisiveness, embrace humility, nurture empathy, and build trust. Recognize the art of knowing when to adapt, when to delegate, and when to make people feel safe. Understand that accomplishment is not solely measured in riches but also in the fulfillment of a meaningful purpose and existence.

Your path to success, like the stories we've explored, is unique to you. I deeply hope that this book helps to create a life filled with more purpose, more wisdom, and the ever-present pursuit of excellence. I wish you well as you continue to build a career and a life remembering these Immortal Truths.